DAVID DILLARD-WRIGHT, PhD

A MINDFUL DAY

365 Ways to Live Life with *Peace, Clarity,* and an *Open Heart*

Adams Media
New York London Toronto Sydney New Delhi

Adams Media
An Imprint of Simon & Schuster, Inc.
57 Littlefield Street
Avon, Massachusetts 02322

First Adams Media trade paperback edition DECEMBER 2017

ADAMS MEDIA and colophon are trademarks of Simon and Schuster.

For information about special discounts for bulk purchases, please contact Simon & Schuster Special Sales at 1-866-506-1949 or business@simonandschuster.com.

The Simon & Schuster Speakers Bureau can bring authors to your live event. For more information or to book an event contact the Simon & Schuster Speakers Bureau at 1-866-248-3049 or visit our website at www.simonspeakers.com.

Interior design by Stephanie Hannus

Interior images © Getty Images and 123RF

Manufactured in China

10 9 8 7 6 5 4 3 2

Library of Congress Cataloging-in-Publication Data has been applied for.

ISBN 978-1-5072-0266-1
ISBN 978-1-5072-0267-8 (ebook)

For all those who seek a better way.

Contents

Acknowledgments

As we come to the third and final book in this series, I am grateful for the friends and family who have sustained and inspired me. Thanks to the Dillards and the Wrights and my own three wild children, Atticus, Oscar, and Tallulah. Thanks to Jess for making these good dreams come true. I want to especially mention the USC Aiken Mindfulness Meditation Group, which gave me many much-needed midday pauses. Once again, thanks to everyone at Adams Media, especially Eileen, Laura, and Bethany. Thanks to that great "cloud of witnesses" ever present with me, giving me inspiration when I didn't know what to say. Thanks to Swami Satyananda Saraswati and Shree Maa of Kamakhya, my living gurus, who inspire my writing and teaching.

Introduction

A Mindful Day explores what we usually consider the main part of the day—the world of work and productivity. I will lead you on an extended meditation that threads its way along a sort of ridgeline toward the summit of peak productivity and deep fulfillment. While walking this ridgeline, you will navigate your way past two precipices, or a set of dualisms that often disturb our thoughts about work: one is heedless neglect, and, the other, an all-consuming frenzy. The consumer cultures in which we live teach, through an unofficial curriculum of books and movies, magazine articles, and television shows, that we must either be frantic workaholics or broke indigents. Given these two bad choices, most of us stumble along, not knowing how to respond. Most of us don't want to be on either end of that spectrum—happiness lies somewhere in the middle.

We must get beyond this all-or-nothing thinking, this excluded middle, this *either-or* that steals the joy from life. Mindfulness means seeing clearly, and it does not serve you or others to see people in terms of the labels of *haves* and *have nots*. And, in order to be fair to ourselves, we need to find a path to productivity that does not steal our souls or our dreams.

We need a way of life that harmonizes our idealist selves with our practical selves, so that we can have the means of life while also having lives. We have to hold to our youthful beliefs in a more just and inclusive world order while also taking care of our responsibilities as employees, parents, friends, and relatives. We have to find the middle way of Aristotle and the Buddha, neither the path of least resistance nor the path of self-harm. And we also have to keep ever mindful of the passing of our days, knowing that everything changes, that we, too, change. So we must learn to be grateful and gracious in the midst of all these changes. This may sound like a tall order—almost impossible, even—but hope and faith require us to seek the unknown way, a genuine path to fulfillment that still allows the "bread *and* roses" of the labor rallying cry. With a great deal of diligence and introspection, we can find this hidden path that leads to the summit. No one can really teach this path, because it is different for each individual, but you can at least find a few clues in these pages.

What Is a Mindful Life?

Before we can begin to focus on practical matters, we must first engage in a little bit of philosophy. Too much labor in this world goes wasted for lack of clear understanding. Imagine someone who walks very industriously but with a faulty compass. Just having that compass off by a few degrees could mean missing the target by a wide margin. Or worse yet, having no compass at all could lead to walking in circles!

Let us suppose that, like the magnetic field of the earth, we have with us all the time a guidance system in the form of intuition. Let us suppose that our hopes and dreams provide us with guidance, and that even our dislikes and complaints have something to offer. The philosopher David Hume said that reason and what he called sentiment were equally valuable in living the moral life. We have to be intelligent, yes, but we also should be emotionally stirred when we see suffering or come across a great work of art. We have to align the head and the heart in order to live in a good way.

In asking how to live mindfully, we are really seeking answers to the old question of what makes for a good human life. I don't believe there is only one way of living a good human life, but many good ways of living as a human being. We have to hold on to our individuality while also keeping in mind our common lot as terrestrial mammals, needing love and support, food, air, and water. Reflecting on what we consider to be good can be one way to escape the treadmill of working to live and living to work. We also have to know why we are living. That is, we must have at least some sense of the reason why we do what we do. The *why* can be otherworldly and metaphysical, or it can be this-worldly and finite. Regardless, we all need a why. The *why* can be implicit or explicit, but it's pretty hard to get out of bed without one. Even though there are no wrong whys in the grand scheme of things, there are ways of living that lead to less suffering or more suffering. For our own sakes and for the sake of those who share the world with us, we should look for the most efficient way of life, the life that provides a sense of well-being without getting into the competitive mindset of eat or be eaten.

Mindfulness As a Way of Life

Even though mindfulness and meditation should not take the place of physical exercise or the advice of your physician, these practices do very good things for your mind and body. You can find in meditation a way to reduce stress, improve sleep, lower blood pressure, and experience many other positive effects, all without taking a pill or going bankrupt in the process. Meditation has now gone completely mainstream, but it can still be intimidating to get started. There are so many different schools of thought, so many different techniques and practices. This plethora of knowledge, so easily accessible, makes it confusing both for beginning and experienced practitioners to know how to optimize the benefits of meditation.

One thing that is clear is that we have to set aside time each day in order to get something out of the practice. This series of books does some of that work for you by having one book dedicated to the morning, one book dedicated to the evening, and this third book dedicated to the daytime. You can find a meditation for any time of day that works for you. Even setting aside, say fifteen or twenty minutes a few times a day will lead to increased concentration, stress reduction, and a greater sense of well-being. You may still have all of the same problems in life, but with the help of meditation they will not affect you to the degree that they once did. You will be able to face obstacles without getting into a frantic state of mind.

Once you have this base practice down, you will want to begin meditating everywhere: while writing a report at work, standing in the line at the supermarket, picking kids up from school, and so forth. This is what is called mindfulness, as opposed to meditation, which we often consider to be a seated practice. Mindfulness is not "spacing out"—just the opposite. The purpose of mindfulness is to pay attention to our lives as much as possible. You will soon come to realize just how difficult this can be in today's society, which is based on distraction as a way of life. Difficult and yet not difficult at all: we are just after a greater connection to the people around us, to the natural world, and to our own inner lives.

How to Use This Book

The book, like its companions *A Mindful Morning* and *A Mindful Evening*, is designed to be read one entry per day. But don't get too fixated on this method: feel free to peruse this book and glean here and there. The important thing is to pause to collect yourself in the middle of the day. By pouring all of your energy into these little meditations, you will come to have a greater appreciation for the time that you have, whether it is a lot or a little. The physical aspect of meditation can be missed easily. If sitting still isn't working for you (and at some point, it won't), go outside for a walk. Get some markers and draw. Pick up a musical instrument. Do something that makes you feel silly. An excess of seriousness can become a serious spiritual problem. If your face has frozen into a frown, then you have to do some serious play to dislodge those frown muscles, that furrowed brow. There will be time enough for serious study and meditation, for hard work and sacrifice. You will know when you have hit a dead end, and, at that point, you have to change things up.

Allow your heart and mind to synchronize with your life's work. Bring yourself back to the here and now as you take time to rest and reflect. You can do this in as little as five minutes, but you can also take an hour or two. Use the time that you have, treasuring every second. You will begin to have more gratitude for every person, thing, and situation in your life, even the difficult ones. By setting aside this little bit of time during your day, *all* of your time will come to seem sacred.

Aversion and Excitement

Every day, every moment, is a new chance to begin again. I have not lost anything, for, in this moment, the possibilities lie open to me.

Today you find before you easy tasks and difficult tasks, things that produce aversion and things that arouse excitement. As you go through this day, whether you do something you like or something you dislike, keep your heart about you. Do not let yourself run away with resentment or anger. Do not let yourself run away with pleasure or distraction, either. The calm heart does not run nor does it tarry. Stay here with yourself, in the present. Be mindful in all that you do.

As you pause to be present in the middle of the day, consider whether any of these aversions or exciting moments could be viewed as new beginnings in your life. Pour your heart's intention into these new beginnings, whether they pertain to home, work, or leisure. Fill these openings of opportunity with goodwill. Wish for these new beginnings to prosper, for good things to arise out of today's efforts, for every ounce of effort to reach its full conclusion. Resolve to see every good thing reach its full expression in your life.

The Power of Action

I have within me the ideas that I need to change my world for the better. I take my divinely guided creativity and put it to work this day.

You have all the inspiration you need to improve your life. You can improve your relationships, your finances, your career, your health, and anything you may wish to change. Stop the rumination and act. Stop planning and act. Stop weighing the options and act. Stop making lists and act. Stop prioritizing and act. A little bit of doing will be more worthwhile than sitting in indecision, which is actually a soothing, comforting enemy-in-disguise. It is better to take the wrong action than to do nothing at all.

Perhaps as you read these lines, your heart leaps at something left undone. Maybe you put something that really matters to you on the back burner. Delay kills all plans. Better to be foolish and alive than to be prudent and embalmed. Go ahead and give five minutes, ten minutes, an hour, a day to the life of your dreams. This is your engraved invitation to a more abundant life.

Interconnectedness

I am not alone or lonely. I belong to the community of things, to the network of other minds. My thoughts belong to the world and return to the world, and I truly belong to the universe.

Your mind does not stop at the confines of your skull but drifts around in the world, interacting with the sensations that come your way—from distant countries, from long-dead authors, from other galaxies. The mind extends to the stars and back again, looping through palaces and gardens, past the smell of your grandmother's perfume and your grandfather's cigars. The mind goes downward into the cells of the body and the interactions of invisible bacteria. We all belong to one big tangle of interconnected threads, one big mind that encompasses everything.

You may find yourself thinking sometimes that you have a zone of privacy, an enclosure of consciousness that no one else can penetrate. And this creates a feeling of isolation and separation. Today, think of the boundaries of the body as transparent and porous, and allow the world to flow through you. See if you feel a sense of release as you step away from isolation.

One-Pointed Attention

In my heart of hearts lies the secret treasure. I will express the best that I have within me with everything that I do and say.

Better does not equal more. To do your best today, you do not need to work yourself to exhaustion or to outcompete your coworkers. Nor do you need to be idle or lazy. Do not judge your efforts at all, either against your own previous efforts or of those around you. Just build your inner fire and work steadily. Put more heart into what you do, even if your work is trivial or repetitive. Each small action becomes a prayer or mantra.

Sit still for a few minutes, closing your eyes if you can, focusing your attention on the ajna chakra between the brows. Put everything you have into remaining fixed on this one spot. You will be tempted to break your concentration nearly constantly, but just remained fixed, with a laser-like intensity, on this one spot. When it is time to go back to your work, maintain this one-pointed (one focus) attention on whatever you happen to be doing at the time. Note the qualitative change that happens with focused work, as opposed to the usual, scattered half-attention.

Difficult Emotional States

In the middle of the day, I look for those things that bind me, preventing me from expressing my full potential. I move myself and my society into more positive directions, living into the immense power of this present moment.

We inherit deep-seated beliefs from our parents, and we also develop mental habits from traumatic events that occurred during childhood. Sometimes our mental predispositions seem so deep-seated that it's impossible to imagine them ever changing. To dislodge deep-seated negative states of mind, we have to look at our larger cultural inheritance, the karma of our entire society, instead of just our own personal rights and wrongs. Depression and anxiety, pessimism and despair, make perfect sense when seen in the light of the destructive tendencies of consumer civilization.

Difficult emotional states like these have a sacred function: they can teach us if we are willing to listen. They cry to us to change our lives and society as well. As you observe your thoughts and emotions today, you may see a persistent pattern that recurs. Look for the hidden message that the difficult emotion might be trying to communicate. Your heart may be crying for change in some area of your life, or it may be asking you to undertake a task on behalf of the world.

Mystery in the Mundane

Beneath name and form is the timeless infinite.
I live for the realization of the divine mystery.

For some reason unknown to us, we have a world before our eyes that, due to the prejudices of our culture, we regard as "material" in nature. For some reason, we find ourselves engaged in various projects and plans, some new and some inherited from the past. None of us chose this for ourselves, at least not in any sense that we are aware. We don't choose to be born. And yet we are forced, just by nature of being alive, to make decisions about our lives. We have to act in some way or another, and even sitting still is a kind of action. Since we are alive, and since we have to choose, we might as well maximize the time that we have here.

Right now, you may see various mundane objects arrayed around you: the table, the desk, the lamp, the couch. You may be aware of your hands holding this book or reader, of your eyes scanning the page. You may have various thoughts and feelings coming and going. Realize that all of this is nothing other than the divine Self, that all becomings belong to the one Being. You are this divinity unfolding in time.

The Human Animal

I commit myself to the practice, whether I find great flashes of inspiration or sit with my perplexity. I acknowledge what I do not know, and I sit here in all my partiality and incompleteness.

As spiritual seekers and as students of philosophy, we have accustomed ourselves to looking for great moments of illumination, flashes of inspiration. This actually becomes an addictive tendency, the need for the next fix. We neglect the silences, the places of murkiness, the negative spaces of the self. It's a much better choice to get comfortable with our ignorance, to stop filling in the blanks of the unknown with prefabricated solutions. I, of course, don't mean the rank kind of ignorance (of the basic facts of science and history, etc.), but the good, purposeful kind of ignorance, which frees us from easy solutions to complex problems.

Today, realize that you will face certain problems as a human being. Among these are pain, aging, disease, and death. You will also experience turbulent emotions, like sadness, anger, joy, and the like. As long as they are appropriate to the situation and kept in proportion, there is nothing wrong with negative or reactive emotions. We should not try to fix the human condition, nor should we despise the so-called *animal* states. Sit here for a few minutes in the darkness, changing nothing, improving nothing. Just be a quiet, terrestrial mammal, breathing in and out.

Go and Be, Go and Do

I live with the past every day, but I need not let it determine me.
I continue to believe in the possibility of new life. With great intelligence,
courage, and strength, I forge a new future for myself and others.

Twitch your little finger, and the planets change in their courses. You may think you do not have this god-like power, but you, my friend, are made of decayed stardust, and you are the culmination of billions of years of experimentation. Your every effort ripples outward in a thousand ways, transforming the world around you. You have already changed the world by opening your eyelids. You are immeasurably great and tremendously powerful. So go and do, go and be, and do not fear making mistakes. You couldn't be more perfect.

Before you go back to being your amazing self, sit here for a few minutes of rest. Allow the tension and worry to dissolve. Stop chastising yourself with critical thoughts. Stop thinking you haven't done enough, that you haven't been enough. Take your leave of the mental turbulence and nurture the peace that you already have within you. Let it grow and grow, and let the disturbance fade away. Let yourself be awash in peace, as you sit and as you rise.

Luminous Inner Space

I find in my heart the source of all inspiration. I do not need to solve my problems through overthinking or ceaseless toil. The correct course of action unfolds automatically. I only need to go along with my inner guide, and everything will be accomplished naturally.

When the mind grows tired of continual effort, we can always take a step back and get in touch with the heart center through deep breathing and meditative awareness. The heart chakra balances masculine and feminine forces, the life of the mind and the life of the emotions. It also balances the left and right side of the body. Breathing into the heart center and concentrating our attention in the heart, we release ourselves from the mental side of life, from the internal dialogue.

As you breathe and move your awareness into the heart center, notice the feeling of relaxation as you turn your attention away from the head region. The inner monologue may continue, but it is now on the periphery of awareness. You become more aware of the interior space. You sense the inner space expanding, then becoming transparent and luminous. Finally, you see that the inner space contains the outer space as well. Your heart opens to the universe, on all beings and all places. You carry a great treasure in your heart: all the worlds and all the beings in them.

Stop Measuring, Start Living

I am not the author of my life. My life does not belong to me. I greet today as a gift and join with this day in joy. I do not seek to conquer or to possess these hours, but to go with them wherever they might lead.

Some self-help books and business books are filled with muscular, aggressive advice. We are told to make lists of goals and set timetables. We are told to keep track of every minute of time, every step of exercise, every business contact. We are told to use specialized software to measure ourselves and automate every aspect of life. So it's no wonder that we fail to pay attention to the great danger of managing ourselves out of existence, of compressing our lives to the point where there is nothing left but more to-do lists. Eventually a breakdown occurs.

Maybe today you don't feel like doing anything at all. You can fight against this impulse to simply stop for a long time, but eventually it will catch up with you. Take a little time right now to rest and recover, to remember your true purpose. You may have a fatigue that goes beyond just being tired: your exhaustion may be a deep sacred yearning for something more. The voice inside you may be the voice of self-preservation, the voice of sanity, the voice of life itself.

No Labels

*I sit in solemn stillness and the world hums with the great presence.
I only listen and keep my mind and heart open. I contribute only my
attention, only this expectant waiting.*

Maybe you have had bad experiences of God in the past, as a result of scary stories told to you as sacred scripture. You may picture God as a vengeful judge, as a stern taskmaster, as a jealous spouse. Perhaps this picture of God led you to abuse yourself or to suffer from abuse inflicted on you by others. After a great amount of time spent in healing, you may see a new picture of God emerging, and maybe you can't even tolerate the word "God" anymore. You sense a benevolent spirit or spirits: you begin to wonder if maybe the cosmos is a hospitable place after all. You give yourself the freedom to worship new gods, to craft beliefs of your own.

Today, as you sit in silence, avoid the temptation to label your experience. Forget about what you may know of world religions and philosophies. Do not try to make your time of meditation conform to what you have learned from other people. Try as hard as you can to set the script aside, to meet whatever you find here in this hour. Listen and pay attention: do not interpret or describe. Worry about what it all means later; for now just be alive in this moment.

The Power to Overcome Negative Circumstance

When I have truly come to the end of my rope, I need only put down my foot and say, "This will be no more." I have the power to begin and the power to end, the power to say yes and the power to say no.

Twelve-step literature recounts experiences of *hitting bottom* as the turning point for getting on the program and getting sober. Some people do need to let things get really bad before they have the strength to find a better way. But we don't need to wait until we are literally lying in the gutter to end the negative tendencies in our lives. We can start today, right now, even if we consider ourselves to be normally functioning members of society. Nearly everyone has some addictive traits; nearly everyone is attached to some*one*, some*thing*, or some *habit*. We begin to end these attachments as soon as we become aware of them and start trying to end them.

You likely have in your life today some consistent complaint, a negative circumstance that you view as the bane of your existence. Part of this may genuinely be out of your control, but you also have great power to transform your experience. Stop looking at the problem through the viewpoint of limitation and lack. See what resources are at your disposal to change things for the better. Make a list of ten things you can do to change your circumstances, and pick a few of them to do today.

The Momentum of Thought

I fully open myself to the possibility that this day brings. I put all of my energy into making new pathways of opportunity in my life.

Thought has a momentum of its own, and we all have habitual ways of thinking called *vrittis*, or mental modifications. Swami Sivananda, in a little book called *Thought Power*, compared these mental patternings to the grooves in a vinyl record. The thoughts continue as before, impelled by the channel that has already been cut in the substrate. And yet the needle can move: we can switch tracks. We can begin a new groove, but it does take some serious effort to overcome the old ways. This happens by deliberately and steadfastly leading the mind down a more positive path.

Optimism doesn't come easily for most people, because it can feel naive or simple-minded to be optimistic in the face of the serious problems facing the planet. And yet, because of the self-perpetuating nature of thought, optimistic thoughts lead to more expansive possibilities, beginning with the mind and then radiating outward into lived reality. Think today about some discouraging situation in your life. Will yourself, through a strenuous effort, into seeing possibility and promise where you previously felt hopeless.

Letting Go of Language

I look within, beyond my personality, to the pure light being that illuminates the world. I allow the inner light to dissolve all confusion, all worry, and all doubt.

We can express thoughts elegantly or badly. We can have highly refined philosophical dialogue, or we can utter drunken babble. Either way, we remain within the self-referential domain of language, words referencing other words. In order to have direct experience, we have to hold language in suspension. If you shake a snow globe, the little fake flurries obscure the scene within, but if you let them settle, you can see clearly. Just so, language obscures both the inner and outer landscape.

As language users and lovers of language, we can be seduced by words, especially our own inner monologues. To let go of these inner thoughts, we must take a step back and watch them. Today, for a few minutes, watch the thoughts like you would watch the snow in the globe, and, as you watch them, see if they begin to settle. Take note of the cruel and jealous thoughts, and the kind ones as well. See them arrayed before you, and notice that you do not control them. Do not stir them; allow them to move into a calmer state.

Patience and Faith

I sit enthroned upon the lotus on the waters of infinite consciousness.
The serpent power coils around me and through me. My meditation carries
me to the supreme one, and I merge into the supreme one.

Two attitudes take us away from realization. First, we insist on a prede-termined outcome for our actions: I want this and only this, and I want it now. This is a kind of childish petulance that is all too common in full-grown adults. A kid asks for candy; adults ask for promotions and raises, fast cars, and big houses. Even highly spiritual people ask for "candy": I want this or that ecstatic state, this or that revelation, and I want it now. The other kind of attitude is a dullness or lassitude, in which I cling to inaction, failing to exert myself at all.

As Shirdi Sai Baba said, we have to develop *nishta*, faith, and *saburi*, patience, while keeping the goal fully in mind and working in accordance with it. Sit for a while, and notice the impatient, anxious thoughts as well as the dull, self-pitying thoughts. Reject both of these and allow patience and faith to bloom in your heart. Picture your own idea of infinite goodness and allow it to fill your mind and heart.

Breath of the Spirit

I breathe the breath of life. I contemplate the breath of life.
I awaken the breath of life. My breath is the breath of the world,
and the breath of the world is my breath.

The ancient Greek word *pneuma* meant breath as well as spirit. The Sanskrit word *prana* means breath, but it also refers to a hidden vital essence. Taoist yoga similarly cultivates the *chi*, in part through breath work. In fact, most traditional cultures around the world have accorded a great importance to the breath and endowed it with cosmic significance. Only in recent centuries have we come to view breathing as a mere exchange of gases.

There are many complex modes of *pranayama*, or breath work, but one can reap most of the benefits simply by breathing more deeply than normal. Try lengthening your inhalation and exhalation to twice the normal rate, not only in duration but also in volume. Keep doing this for a few minutes. Picture yourself breathing not only air but also a hidden vital energy that flows throughout your surroundings.

Cultivating Peace
and Goodwill

*I let go of the need to conform to the expectations that others have of me.
I let go of the expectations that I have for the way that other people will
behave toward me. I accept the reality around me and release the need for it
to be this way or that.*

We create our own mental knots by cultivating outrage over the smallest slight. We mentally play the same scenes of victimhood and grievance over and over again, the same tired scenes, the same script. We don't need to buy into a grand metaphysical theory of karma in order to improve our lot; we just have to get tired of making ourselves miserable. We have to make a conscious choice to do things differently. That different way of doing things lies in simply refusing to get bent out of shape, and in purposely cultivating feelings of peace and goodwill. Over a long period of time, with a lot of practice, the old mental patterns begin to realign.

In this midday break, perhaps you can recall a time today when you nursed a sense of grievance or outrage. Take the time now to forgive the person who you think did you wrong. Maybe the word "forgive" is too strong: just notice the mental tangle that you caused for yourself. Notice that the reactionary mental state is separate from the incident that gave rise to it. Wind down the anger and resentment. Breathe calm into the tortured mind.

Alive and Free at Work

My being resonates with the divine essence that fills the universe. Beneath my personality, my thoughts, and my emotion lies the timeless infinite. When I work from this place of deep and abiding calm, all things fall into place.

You have been conditioned to believe that adult life must always be stressful, must always be a struggle. You may even be afraid to smile, lest your coworkers think you are not pulling your weight. Recognize this dour-countenanced drudgery as a sort of pose or sham. You can have a calm, peaceful, joyous heart and still be perfectly productive. You can let down your guard every now and then and not get eaten alive. As you allow yourself more freedom to express your true self, you give that same freedom to everyone you meet. And the work gets a little easier and a little more fun.

What would happen if you were to laugh and smile at work? What would happen if you did not complain even once this week? As you look at the thoughts that arise for you, do you detect strains of joylessness? Do one thing today that makes you feel alive and free, something that will not get you fired but is nonetheless fun and interesting. See if you can become a vector for change at your place of work, someone who changes the workplace culture for the better.

A Little Bit of Activity

I have the resources that I need to uphold my fellow travelers on this earth. I support, and I am supported. I serve, and I am served. I love, and I am loved.

Make no mistake about it, it is the demon on your shoulder who tells you that your life does not matter, that you work is meaningless, that no one cares about you. These destructive thoughts are, quite simply, lies, but they can be very persistent. In order to defeat them, you must work very hard in the opposite direction. Pour as much care and concern into your work as possible. There is a real person on the other end of every transaction in the business world. How you do things matters, and no task is inherently meaningless or worthless.

Maybe today you are feeling down, emotionally or physically or both. Give yourself a little bit of grace, but go ahead and accomplish some things, even little things. Do a little bit of organization. Focus on something manageable and easy. If you are able to take a break, write a few pages in your journal or doodle a little picture. Just a little bit of activity will make you feel better. Putting yourself into what you do will make you feel better. Staying with the present moment will make you feel better.

Meditation on White Light

I have within me the increate light of the ages. I have within me all knowledge, all love, and all bliss. I came from the light and return to the light. All things merge into the light.

You may arrive at your meditation space with the best intentions, but some nagging thought just gets in the way. You have a sort of two-track mind, one track that does the practice and another that ruminates on the problem. The first solution should be to take concrete action, but, if you have already done that, how can you make the two-track mind into a one-pointed mind?

Imagine a radiant sphere of white light, centered in your chest region. It expands to include the neck and head. It expands further to encompass your entire body and the place where you are sitting. This light contains all knowledge, all goodness, and, indeed, everything in existence. Build the intensity of this light and increase your awareness of it. Then begin to surrender your problem to the light. Picture this brilliant light of love and knowledge dissolving all obstacles. When you have done this meditation as fully as you can, go back to work. A solution will soon appear.

The Power to Change

I may not have unlimited power, but I lay hold of the power that I do have to change my situation. I look not just to adapt myself to a cruel fate, but, through tremendous force of will, to become one with the divine fire in me.

Judeo-Christian religion tends to emphasize human frailty, the belief that negative tendencies form an ingrained part of human nature. Looking at human history so far, I can certainly understand that point of view. However, I choose to believe that I can overcome sin (literally "missing the mark") through my own effort, and I find this belief to be more inspiring and empowering than the belief that we are helpless over sin. This shift in emphasis has made it possible for me to hold on to both devotional religion and secular knowledge.

Take a look at your own conditioned beliefs. Perhaps you see some ways in which you have been taught to accept a life that is less than your best, because you believe that you simply cannot change. Now imagine for a second that you do have the power to change your habits, your circumstances, and your beliefs. Stay for a moment in a place of suspension, where you put your preconditioned attitudes aside for awhile. Dwell in uncertainty, and, when you are ready, start asking what beliefs and habits might better serve you.

The Magic of Presence

As I look around me, I see the many separate things, but I also strive to see beyond the surfaces to the heart of all reality. I see being in the midst of becoming, the eternal in the midst of time, the divine effulgence in the everyday.

You have come to the exact place in life where you were meant to be. Everything in your life until this point has led to this moment. You may experience your reality as harsh or unforgiving, but there is something here to be learned, something to be gained. Hold on to this moment until it teaches you its lesson. Hold on to this place until it gives you its blessing. Time has depth as well as duration, and, by holding on to this moment in all of its pain and splendor, you receive grace.

Take the time to be fully present in this moment, to everything in your surroundings, to everything in your mind and heart. Feel the twitch of avoidance, the urge to escape into distraction, the urge to flee and fantasize. Ignore the twitch, and go back to the present. Stay with this moment at least until you feel an inner release. Then go back to your work, remaining calm and centered.

Overcoming Hostility

I allow yesterday's reality to fade away.
I allow the passage of time to carry away pain, fear, and grief.

Hostility or enmity toward others shrinks the circle of concern that we have available to meet the challenges of life. Hatred of those who do not share the same ethnicity or religion, the same socio-economic status, the same likes and preferences, leads to a diminished reality, a decrease in personal efficacy and emotional intelligence. Holding grudges from the past also constrains our ability to meet the present in an open manner. We cannot be effective in our working lives or our personal lives if we decide in advance that we will not interact with broad swaths of humanity.

Take a look at your own mental and emotional life today. Have you foreclosed on possibilities for relationship and openness? Do you look down on certain individual people or groups of people? Allow your heart to open once again to those you have neglected or ignored. Allow for at least the possibility of greater openness and communication. Be willing to make the first move toward reconciliation. Drop grudges from the past, and drop the stance of victimhood. Find forgiveness, and claim your own power.

Earth Meditation

The earth supports me and gives me life.
The earth is the context for my hopes and dreams and the source of my
wealth. I honor and cherish the earth, and the earth upholds me.

Life may be abundant in the universe, but, so far as we know, this blue orb in the vastness of space is the only home we may ever have. We may only get one chance as a human species to live here on this beautiful planet that harbors bird and beast and coral reef, one chance to live in this cacophony of life, this riot of color and form, this planet of desert and ocean, steppe and mountain, mesa and plain. This place has been so good to us, and we have taken it for granted, despoiled its beauty, raided its vast storehouses. We must learn, as a species, to once again honor the earth, to come back into a more reciprocal relationship with the source of life.

As you sit here in your meditation space, take a minute to feel gravity rooting you to the earth. Breathe the good air, and feel the atmosphere around you. See the earth's magnetic field surrounding the planet, and see the myriad creatures who call this place home. Allow gratitude for the earth to fill your heart. Take a silent vow to be kind to the earth, to protect the planet from those who would destroy it. Know that as you protect the earth, the earth protects you.

The Next Steps

I let the inner light shine through me. I allow the inner genius to awaken and accomplish its goals through me. I awaken to higher illumination, bringing my work into line with divine guidance.

Inspiration need not be a torturous process: sometimes the right words just come at the right time. Sometimes the next action steps just appear at the right moment. When we feel stalled with our work lives or our creative lives, it is usually because we assume too much of the burden. We think that we have to be brilliant, that we have to be heroic, larger-than-life figures. We think we have to work harder and longer than the next guy. But really all we have to do is get out of the way, to put words to paper or paint to canvas, and let the spirit guide.

Right now, picture everything falling into place. Whatever situation might be bothering you, see the resolution coming quite naturally. You don't need to do a lot of rumination or strategizing: the solutions just appear. The work gets done; the right ideas get turned into a beautiful final product. Sit here for a few minutes in the secure knowledge that everything you need is within arm's reach. Commit yourself to taking only one step at a time. When you leave this time of meditation, you will be presented, in such a simple and natural way, with the next steps that you need to take on your life's journey.

The Call of Curiosity

I open my life to the divine power of curiosity.
My mind and body are renewed as I allow myself to see the bigger picture.
I follow the beckoning of the world around me.

We suffer because we believe that we are the authors of our own lives, because we think we have to wrestle life to the ground and force it to submit to our will. Our adult, overly responsible selves have an overbearing sense of the I. *I* have to go to work. *I* have to pay the bills. *I* have to take care of the children. All the while, we lose the sense of wonder, the sense of life as one big game of hide-and-go-seek with God (or beauty or mystery, or whatever you choose to call it). The sense of adventure and wonder only returns when we allow ourselves to follow the call of curiosity, the beckoning of the world around us.

Today you might be feeling bored, stressed, or exhausted. Your spirit may be flagging, and you may feel a sense of drudgery with regard to work and housework. Look within your mind and heart: you only need one small spark of curiosity or inspiration to keep you going. You need only deviate from your routine a tiny bit in order to feel a sense of newness. See that spark within you now. What is it asking you to do? What new areas await exploration?

The Great Transformation

The treasure lies buried in the field. I do not need to see this treasure to know that it is there. I sell all that I have in order to buy the field.

The private life of my consciousness opens onto the world around me. I am affected by the world, and I affect the world in turn. All around me are new vectors for thought, for willing, for action. As I work and dream and be, I undergo a great transformation. I widen the circle of my concern to encompass people in other lands, to include the nonhuman creatures, to include the natural environment. I do not see myself as standing apart or aloof: I belong to this great unfolding of the patterns of nature. My mind is nothing other than the mind of nature.

Today you may find yourself wanting to cower, wanting to curl into a ball and hide under your desk. You may be sick and tired of dealing with people and problems. Give yourself this moment of rest and renewal, but realize also that the face of a stranger is your own face, that the grass and the trees are the stuff of your dreams. The life that you live in public is the raw material of your inner life, and your inner life is your worldly life inverted. You are this crossing of the inside and the outside, the place where mind and matter meet.

The Three Qualities

I release habits that do not serve me. I release thoughts that do not serve me. I release emotions that do not serve me. I release personality traits that do not serve me. I release beliefs that do not serve me.

Every creative person goes through ups and downs, frenzied bouts of activity followed by troughs of stagnation and depression. These oscillations in energy level are not confined to the human sphere and can be found throughout nature. By understanding the three *gunas*, or qualities, of *rajas* (activity), *tamas* (lethargy), and *sattva* (clarity), highly effective people can propel work forward by using natural cycles as an advantage. Attempting to push through at the wrong moment can lead to premature burnout, while giving in to lethargy can frustrate any effort. The creative spiritual practitioner rides the waves of the gunas while lingering on the liberating quality of sattva.

Which of the three gunas do you think predominates in your life right now? What practices in your life could lead to greater clarity at work or at home? Take a few minutes to jot down a few paragraphs about your present life situation, including any complaints you might have. When you are finished, burn or shred the pages. Make a resolution now to start anew, moving forward with clarity and grace.

The Great Beyond

I allow newness of life to flow through me. I am still being born, even today.
Each new moment is being born right in front of me.
I bind myself to this long, eternal Now.

Any self-help expert today will recommend social networking as a way to sell any product or get ahead in any field. What has been less understood is the true meaning of the "social" as encompassing all orders of nature, from inanimate objects to plants and animals to gods and ancestors. A narrow focus on "social media" or "networking" will pale in comparison to the positive benefits of joining with nature itself to achieve a desired result. Creative spiritual practitioners connect with this great beyond to achieve a more expansive and original result.

If you are feeling stuck in your life right now, it may be that you have cast yourself into a narrow role. Changing your physical habits can help. Go for a walk outside today. Bring a plant into your office. Talk with someone you have never met. Spend some time in silent contemplation. In order to get beyond an impasse, you must get beyond the mindset that created the impasse in the first place. You must open your limited mind to the mind of nature.

Healthy Risk

In the lotus of my heart is a crystal Shiva lingam, a symbol of divine energy that radiates effulgent white light. The light of infinite goodness flows through my heart and throughout my body. I am immersed in this goodness. All things are immersed in this goodness. In truth, no person or circumstance can be separated from infinite goodness.

Most people fear risk, in that it carries the very real possibility of loss. At the same time, risk makes life worthwhile, because we all want to have "stood the test" and live to tell about it. Risk can be something small, like buying a lottery ticket, or large, like skydiving, but no life is really complete without it. Everyone who feels "stuck" in life has some form of risk aversion that prevents them from exploring new possibilities in life. Creative spiritual practitioners recognize risk as a friend in disguise, waiting to take them to unseen possibilities.

If you believed that the universe and other people were basically good and trustworthy, how would that change your attitude toward risk? Is your attitude toward risk one of healthy discernment, or is it a more negative one of cowering in fear? As you go through the rest of the day, see if some small, calculated risk can move you forward in the direction you want to go in life.

Healing the Divide

I honor my body, my mind, and my spirit. I will not do violence to my body, my mind, or my spirit. I look for ways to sustain my body, my mind, and my spirit.

The Western world has developed, with only a handful of exceptions, in the belief that spirit and matter must be forever separate and antagonistic in their relationship to each other. This has given most Westerners terrible phobias of bodily existence, a horrible attitude toward the earth and animals, and a poor understanding of the emotional and intuitive aspects of intelligence. If we can think of God and matter as coinciding, of spirit and flesh as aspects of one reality, then it becomes possible to heal the harmful divisions that have damaged us as people. As we heal ourselves, we also work for more just societies that properly honor and respect nonhuman nature as a manifestation of the divine. Perhaps you find yourself faced with a choice between physical well-being and the life of the spirit. Maybe you feel torn between the practical and the spiritual. Hold open a place of possibility for a solution that honors both the needs of the body and the life of the spirit. Sit in an attitude of hopeful awaiting, and allow for the dawning of a new way. Prepare your heart and mind for this opening in your life, the harmonization of matter and spirit.

Accepting Change

I accept that which remains with me and that which passes away.
I give thanks for that which remains with me and that which passes away.
I love that which remains with me and that which passes away.

Everything must one day come to an end, and yet endings surprise us all the time: a friend moves out of town; the much-loved restaurant closes down; the secure job gets liquidated. Everything is in the process of coming-to-be and no-longer-being: the universe grants no exemptions. In the dharmic worldview, mortals may even become gods and gods may become mortals. Not even divine beings are granted complete immunity from the process of change. We cannot get rid of change, but we can keep change in mind. The plus side of this continual flux is that even circumstances we consider negative must necessarily come to an end.

Think of a few things that have changed in your life recently. See where you may be having trouble accepting change and take a few minutes to reflect on your resistance. Breathe into those sticky places and see if you can find some small place of release. You need not let go all at once, and it will do no good to pretend things are okay if they really are not. Ease yourself, little by little, into a place of greater acceptance.

The Mystery of This Moment

*I begin anew this moment. I awaken to the possibility
that this moment holds. I live into this unknown present.
I do not reduce the present to my preconceived notions.*

The ego nature already knows everything and therefore can never experience anything new or surprising. The ego nature is the lesser self, because it limits the range of possible experiences open to us as human beings. To fully experience this full range of possibilities, we must have humility, which arises when we admit that we do not know it all. Humility arises when we wait for the possibility of something genuinely new in the encounter with the other.

Practice seeing this moment as absolutely new and unique in the history of the universe. Think of the billions of years of cosmic change that have led to your presence in this place and time. Think of the many opportunities that have led you to this place in your life's journey. Think of the struggles that have brought you to this place in your life. This moment is worth savoring, because so much has gone into making it possible. Cherish these few moments of quiet as something precious, unfathomably unique, like precious gems. Live into the mystery of this moment, and see what awaits you here.

Cutting Through
the Word Cloud

I trace thoughts back to their source. I find no support for them.
Thoughts lead only to other thoughts. These thoughts flow through me,
but they are not me. I let them come and go, unimpeded.

We live our lives in a cloud of words: little tidbits of the day's news, habitually recalled memories, plans and schemes for the situation at hand. The word cloud comes to seem more real than the actual reality in front of our faces. We become so habituated to our internal monologues that we hardly notice that they obscure our vision of the present. To reconnect with the present, we have to see through the ready-made filters of language and once again pay attention to reality.

As you close your eyes in meditation, pay attention to the outlines of your body, and allow yourself to settle into the inner darkness. Feel yourself firmly rooted into your seat, and allow energy to move up your spine as you breathe deeply. When you reach the point between your eyebrows, fix your inner gaze here with single-pointed attention. Allow the thoughts to dissolve before the firmness and intention of your one-pointed devotion. Feel the inner space expand to include your surroundings. Know that all things can be represented here within, but be content to sit in darkness and not-knowing. Sit here in the murky darkness until you feel a palpable sense of release.

Right Effort

I give myself the freedom to be who I am today, without judgment or blame.
I give myself to this moment, calmly and purposefully. I keep myself poised
and alert, neither falling into lethargy nor pushing into aggression.

You may catch yourself from time to time desiring to be a "great person," a world-changing, larger-than-life figure, someone who makes a difference in world history. This could lead you to strive harder, which serves as a remedy for lethargy and depression. But the desire to be a great transformative leader is still an attachment, a manifestation of ego. To release this desire, try to let go of the future and think only about today. Do your daily allotment of work, of meditation, of caring, of service, of exercise, and leave the rest to God or the universe. You cannot control how you will be judged by history; you can only do your daily rounds.

Think for a few minutes about exerting the right amount of effort today. Too little effort will undermine every single one of your goals, while too much effort will prematurely exhaust you and lead to dissatisfaction. What would it look like today to exert yourself the right amount in mindfulness, in work, in play, in sociability? Try to find that balance as you go through the rest of your day.

Pushing Beyond Boredom

If I cannot find what I want inside myself, I will not be able to find it anywhere. If I cannot find peace here and now, I will not be able to find it anywhere. I open my heart to contentment and peace in this place and at this time, so that I can carry it with me wherever I go.

After getting into the habit of daily meditation, you may start to lose a sense of magic or fulfillment in the practice. You may feel robotic while saying your mantras or sitting in your asana (yoga posture). You may feel extreme boredom punctuated by bouts of frustration or even rage. This dryness results from the expansion of your previous capacities: you begin to have this dull feeling when you have pushed yourself to the limit. Work with spiritual dryness the way that a marathon runner pushes through "the wall." Attend to the discomfort in the same way that you would attend to any thought or sensation that arises in meditation.

You may feel very strongly right now a temptation to abandon the practice. Ask yourself: what am I running from? Why is it so uncomfortable to be with myself? Why is it so uncomfortable to sit here in silence? What do I hope to gain by leaving? I come home to myself now. I become simultaneous with myself. I release the desire to escape.

The Blessing of Silence

I let go of the trivial rewards of procrastination and bind myself to the pain and joy of this present moment. I rivet my attention to this moment, making myself available to what I find here and now.

Distraction promises a quick fix of fleeting amusement, but, in the end, it proves to be a false friend. Distraction saps the vitality out of life, making a ruin of any plan that requires more than five minutes of preparation. Our little avoidance strategies seem harmless in the moment, but they rob us of good timing, the ability to strike while the iron is hot. Our creative projects die for lack of effort and attention, and then we go around feeling irritable at the lack of positive development. Better to put aside distraction at least until some good work has been accomplished. Better to face the pain of uncertainty than to yield to temporary pleasure.

Take a minute or two to close your Internet browser and turn off your phone. See what it feels like to sit here without the web and social media. Notice any feelings of anxiety that may arise. Do not yield to the fear that you will miss something. Stay here with the silence until it gives you its blessing.

Inner Intentions and Outward Actions

I will not use my spiritual practice as an excuse for not taking pragmatic action to change my life. I will use my spirituality to create visions for change. I then exercise all of my faculties to make my desired way of life a reality.

Spirituality can be either a positive force of self-empowerment or a negative force of self-abasement; it all depends on the attitude of the individual practitioner. Spirituality becomes damaging when it serves as a substitute for actions that might otherwise be taken to improve the situation. Rather than praying to lose weight, it would be better to exercise and eat a proper diet. Of course these are not either/or propositions: in the best-case scenario, inner intentions and outward actions are perfectly aligned.

Have you ever felt like you didn't get the desired result from prayer or mantra practice? Looking back on the situation, did you do enough through simple effort to change the situation? Taking a look at your life right now, identify some ways that you can address your complaints through concrete action. Then, rather than solely asking for things through prayer/meditation, give thanks for the positive changes that you see happening in your life.

Focusing on the Possible

I will do my daily allotment of work, keeping my life's mission always in mind. I will not work myself to death, nor will I fail to exercise my talents.

Not everyone who tries really hard succeeds, and not everyone who succeeds tries really hard. That is to say that some individuals work like dogs their entire lives and don't get anywhere, while others are born into wealth (or fame and privilege) or simply get lucky. It can be easy to fixate on the unfairness of it all and simply give up any hope of creating a better life for ourselves, to slide into passive resignation. But this depressive, forlorn attitude (which sometimes masquerades as spirituality) does not improve life one iota. In fact, it can lead to missing opportunities that could otherwise be used to great advantage in improving quality of life. We have to focus on what lies within our control and forget about the rest.

Today, allow thoughts of success to fade into the background. It is all well and good to visualize your ideal future, but it is better to concentrate instead on what can be done today in order to live the way that you want to live. After a few minutes of clearing away the distracting thoughts, make a list of the true action items, those tasks that are both achievable and in line with your life's mission.

Victory to the Divine Mother

The mother of all things waits for me. She fills my heart with treasures of joy and gratitude. She welcomes me home and binds my wounds. She commands the demons, and they depart. Victory to the Divine Mother!

We have a place of refuge with us all the time. In this still place, this fortress within, lies all peace and contentment and every joy conceivable for humankind. We just need to believe that such a place exists, banish all contrary thoughts, and turn our minds to the inner darkness. We have nothing to lose but our illusions and evasions. The techniques for opening this inner space can be elaborate or simple: we just need to find what works and keep returning to this calm center of our being.

Even as you read these words, you may find yourself disbelieving that such a place of refuge exists. Flag each contrary thought as a lie or delusion, and then let it go. Allow yourself *only* the thought of a benevolent Divine Mother, who is waiting to dispel all doubt and welcome you home. Give yourself to the opening of the interior space, and allow this darkness-that-is-light to consume all negativity and grief. If you can do this once, you can do it a thousand times. If you can do this a thousand times, you will be truly free.

The Five-Letter Mantra

The poison of grief has been swallowed.
I enter into the bliss that unfolds for me.
I release my sorrow as I bathe in the divine nectar.

You may now and then feel that your meditation is not working, that all has been for naught, that you are the same person you have always been. Recognize this line of thinking as an evasion. Redouble and triple your efforts. Take meditation and mindfulness from being a passing interest to the central aim and purpose of your life. Make work into mindfulness and play into mindfulness. Learn the mantras and the sutras, the sacred scriptures that teach the way. Seek the advice of a qualified teacher. Once you do this, liberation is near at hand. You can be truly free in this lifetime: reach out and grasp it!

Today, practice the five-syllable (holy five-letter) mantra (from the five Sanskrit letters that comprise it): *aum namah shivaya*. The five syllables are na-mah shi-va-ya, with the holy *aum*, which stands for creation, preservation, and destruction, standing apart. This is a mantra to Shiva, who is the Lord of Infinite Goodness, who represents the intrinsic goodness of everything in existence. Recognize everything that has happened in your life, everything that is happening now, and everything that will happen as you work toward your realization of infinite bliss. Surrender yourself to the divine reality hidden in this moment as you say the mantra.

Give Everything Away

I am willing to set everything aside so that I can come home to bliss. I let go of my defenses and surrender to the mystery before me. With gratitude I plunge myself into the darkness, knowing that I will emerge more complete.

Some question led you to the practice of meditation. Maybe you have been working through a life transition, looking for improved health, seeking increased concentration, or trying to find meaning in life. The profound beauty of meditation, the one really deep secret, is that the mind finds everything it needs when it becomes completely empty. All the techniques add up to this subtraction of preconceived notions, this loss of every certainty. We find ourselves by giving everything away, by scouring away the mental accretions of the years until the mental landscape is raw and exposed. Bliss comes when everything else has been carted away.

Today, do not be timid or halfhearted. Lengthen your spine and put your whole mind and heart into the practice. Slay every idea that comes before your mind's eye, and be extremely vigilant. Know that peace is coming to you, joy is coming to you, insight is coming to you. Let go of the tethers that bind you to this world and walk into the unknown.

The Song of the Cicadas

I open my mind and heart to the cosmic sound, to which I belong and to which I will return. I do not hold myself apart, but join the song of all existence.

In Plato's *Phaedrus*, the character of Socrates recounts a legend that the cicadas were once human beings. They were so enthralled by the Muses that they kept singing, forgetting to eat, sleep, or drink. They were given the reward of rebirth as cicadas so that they might sing forever. Every time I hear the cicadas in the pine trees of my home state of Georgia, I think about this myth, and about my own guru, who has spent most of his life chanting the Sanskrit mantras. I think also about the one universal song, the melody and harmony in which we all participate, the vibrational aspect of all reality.

Lose yourself in sound today. Think of yourself not as a separate being but as an emanation of the one cosmic sound. This sound extends beyond your physical form and courses through all things. No one knows when it began or when it will end. You cannot stop it or start it; you can only be more or less aware of it.

Local Time and Place

I reconnect with the place where I live. I find my home wherever I happen to be.

My family and I like to go to minor league baseball games—the Augusta GreenJackets home games, to be exact. It feels more real than watching a game on TV or even going to a big league stadium. Even the cheap seats are ten feet from home plate, and you can really hear the crack of the bat and smell the freshly mown grass. The games, too, are more unpredictable: an inning can last five minutes or an hour. It is so good to have a local event that is fun for everyone. Every little place has its hidden gems: we just have to go out and find them.

We have gotten so used to experiencing the world through electronic media that we forget the world right in front of our faces. Get outside for a little while today. Go for a walk in a park or downtown. Experience the sights, sounds, and smells directly. Allow your mind to recharge as you meet reality directly.

The Bonds of Kindness

I extend kindness and compassion to my friends and to my enemies.
I recognize the fragile bonds that hold society together,
and I will do my part today to care for those around me.

When times get truly scary, as in political upheavals and war, drought and disaster, human kindness and concern provide some measure of relief. Caring and compassion really hold the world together, however much politicians and generals may brag and posture about their contributions. When all else fails, we have to remember our basic human kindness. Only then will we find hope. Even in the midst of conflict, compassion makes unlivable situations more bearable.

Today you may find your life fractured in some way by conflict. See if you can reach out to another person, while not necessarily agreeing with their views. Extend a smile or a kind word, share food or drink. Sometimes conflict in society is truly necessary and even good, but, at some point, we all still have to live together. Try to recover the bonds of kindness that may have been lost.

Green Time, Not Screen Time

I take my life back from the digital noise that surrounds me. I become, once again, a creature on the face of the earth, an animal moving through the landscape. I return to earth where I was born, and I release distraction.

Little kids only need a couple of sticks to find a fun game to play—sword fighting, cops and robbers, maybe just digging a hole in the ground. At some point, probably as a result of the failure, as adults, to really connect with nature, our kids lose a desire to collect acorns and rocks. Our kids spend more and more time with games, TV shows, and apps, and less and less time playing in the dirt. It will take decades to sort through the sociological and psychological impact of this shift, but we lose something profound when we do not connect with the natural world.

Today, give yourself a little less screen time and a little more green time. Put down your devices and take an unplugged walk outside. Lie in the grass, sit on the porch, or relax in a hammock. All kinds of alarm bells will sound in your mind about who you should be calling, the work you should be doing. You will jones for your favorite websites and twitch for your social media feeds. Ignore all of these false alerts and give yourself some time in nature. You will feel refreshed mentally and emotionally, and remember what you like about being alive.

One Thing at a Time

I resolve today to do only one thing at a time to the best of my ability.
I resolve to concentrate only on that which is most important.
Properly ordering my priorities, my life becomes more peaceful.

We run into problems in life by trying to do too many things at a time. The only important question is, "What do I need to do right now?" Once that question is answered, it only remains to put full concentration onto that task. It becomes so much easier to work when other concerns have been put aside, when all of our powers come to bear on this one thing. Then our physical and mental selves come into alignment with the task at hand, and things progress smoothly.

You have worked hard today, but have you done the exact thing that you needed to do? Have you been able to put your full powers into the task at hand? As you breathe deeply and close your eyes, ask yourself what one thing, if done today, would make you feel better about your life. Ask yourself what task, once completed, would give you greater peace of mind. After sitting here in silence for a few minutes, dedicate yourself completely to that one most important thing.

Deep Intuition

I trust in my own deepest self. I will not bow to anyone who makes me feel ashamed. I am not inherently sinful, egotistical, or immoral.
I bow to my own deepest wisdom, which is unique in all the universe.

A legitimate philosophy or religion constantly provides internal justification to its adherents by making them feel more fulfilled, complete, and functional. An illegitimate belief system uses external constraints, by meddling in the sexual relationships of believers, by using physical coercion, by intimidating or ostracizing critics. When a movement seeks to draw followers to some transcendent or utopian aim, the stakes get raised immeasurably high. People can and do give their entire lives to false teachers and questionable causes. It takes much courage to leave behind toxic beliefs and launch into the world on the strengths of one's own thinking and intuition.

Perhaps you have been wounded in the past by a false teacher or a false belief system that shattered your self-image, that held you back as a person and took away your free will. Take this time to listen deep within to your own best intuition, to trust that you know what is best for yourself. Feel that intuition leading you into a safe and abundant place in life.

Kindness to the Ego

I see my personality as a guise that I am wearing, and yet I honor my personality. I see my social roles as elaborate fictions, and yet I acknowledge my place in them. I see that I have invented my thoughts and emotions, and yet I give them space to be as they are.

Spiritual practice often begins by presuming that the self or the ego is bad and must be transcended. But the ego or personality also helps us to make narrative sense of the world, to have a sense of grounding and purpose. Rather than seeking to obliterate, repress, or transcend the ego, we can just acknowledge it as a fiction, yes, but a useful fiction. In meditation, we can see clearly—as plain as day—that the self is a fabrication or a construct, but then so is everything else in existence. Perhaps this knowledge can just help us to be more kind, more charitable toward these characters that we have made for ourselves.

Right now, in this quiet time, put down the stick of self-judgment and the cudgel of self-blame. See the things that you have done and said: the good, the bad, and the ugly. Accept everything and judge nothing. See your personality, in a strict sense, as unreal, and yet honor the person you have become.

Desires and Appetites

I acknowledge my desire and do not condemn or repress it.
If I choose to indulge, I do so with my full self, sparing nothing. If I choose
to abstain, I do so with my full self, sparing nothing. Whether indulging or
abstaining, I enter fully into experience, sparing nothing.

What do we make of the cravings for food and drink, for sex and money, for fame and power? Most religions and philosophies in the world teach that such things offer fleeting satisfaction but are inappropriate as guiding aims in life. And yet we admit to having such cravings. Perhaps rather than practicing repression on one side or overindulgence on the other, we can spiritualize desire by becoming mindful of it. If we eat and drink, we should eat and drink with full appreciation and mindfulness. If we have sex, we should do so with full appreciation and mindfulness. And so on. If we become fully immersed in experience, the craving aspect diminishes, and we come into a space of suspension in which the present moment blooms into its fullness and splendor.

Maybe right now you feel some craving. If you are currently at work, you may want something simple like a cup of coffee or a chocolate bar. Go ahead and experience whatever you desire, but experience it fully with all of your faculties. See if you do not experience a subtle transformation as a result of entering fully and completely into the present moment.

Cultivating Perfect Peace

For my own good and for the good of others, I center myself in calm and peace. For my own good and for the good of others, I open myself to the ocean of tranquility. For my own good and for the good of others, I make the mind supple and light.

This afternoon, my supervisor at work will give me an assignment I don't really want. A customer or client will make unreasonable demands on my time. Someone will cut in front of me in traffic on the way home. I can decide ahead of time to meet all challenges calmly, in a spirit of kindness and cooperation. Whether I acquiesce to the demands made of me or resist, I can do so in a tranquil fashion. I can choose a peaceful state of mind, even if I can't control the behavior of other people. I can choose calm in the midst of the turmoil around me.

As you sit here in silence, imagine what a perfect state of mind would be. Imagine perfect peace, perfect goodwill, perfect love and graciousness. Cultivate this state of mind: allow it to expand and become stronger. Imagine this awareness to be so strong that nothing could overcome it or weaken it. Will this state of mind to become real and abiding.

Awareness of Aging and Death

*I allow my pain and suffering to make me more compassionate toward others.
I accept this body, even though it causes me pain and discomfort. I accept my
nature as a creature on this earth, and I embrace all aspects of my journey.*

This body that you have known so well will eventually degrade to some degree. You will have some type pain or disability. Your mind, too, will change. You will forget things, important things, until it seems like there is more forgetting than remembering. You might even feel like a rag doll that has been patched a thousand times, with stuffing for brains. Maybe this has already happened to you, or maybe it is happening slowly and imperceptibly. Medicine and technology may be able to slow this process here and there, but aging and death are still existential realities for us, as they were for the first humans who walked the earth.

This day, you may experience your body as a good and faithful friend, or you may experience it as a hostile force working against you. You may feel very happy about your body, or you may hate your body. Whatever feelings you have, take the time to sit with them at this time. Work toward acceptance of your physical form. Work toward acceptance of pain and disability. Do those things that you can do to improve your situation, but do not torture yourself for what lies beyond your control.

Mindfulness and Social Change

I allow myself to become a vector for change in the world. I make my stand on behalf of the earth, nonhuman creatures, and the powerless among us.

If you are feeling depressed about your life, about the state of the world, that is a sign of sanity and not of mental illness. We live in an upside-down world in which too many greedy, ruthless people are in charge, in which things that matter—like clean air and clean water—are often destroyed in favor of base profit. Do not fear: all things will be set right in the end. All people reap the consequences of their actions in the course of time, and we can all work together to build a better world.

Mindfulness and social change go hand in hand: the meditator comes to care more deeply about other people and the planet. Today, open yourself to the possibility of change. Be willing to work for a better world. As you sit here in silence, ask for the inspiration for one constructive thing that you can do to make the world a better place.

The Paradox of Mastery

I allow myself to begin any new pursuit, without having to be the absolute best in what I do. I surrender perfection and embrace imperfection. I cherish the in-between, the journey, the new beginning.

The word "mastery" produces a variety of stumbling blocks for creative types, entrepreneurs, and really almost anyone trying to do something new and innovative. In order to change the world, we think we must first "master" the subject, field, or area of endeavor. The idea of mastery acts like a double-edged sword, though. Without striving to achieve mastery, it might be impossible to conjure the resolve, drive, and ambition necessary to undertake the work. On the other side, the mastery model creates an unattainable standard of success, one that leads to self-loathing. Golfers look up to Arnold Palmer or Tiger Woods, executives to Jack Welch or Warren Buffett, mystics to Saint Francis or Sri Aurobindo, and so forth. "If I could just achieve that level of play, I could really make it," we think to ourselves.

How have you impeded your own progress by setting unrealistic standards? Today, release your expectations of instant success. Sit here in the silence and cultivate the "beginner's mind." Allow the grandiose visions to exit your consciousness. Feel free to fail. Feel free to stumble and fall. Above all, begin.

Beyond Hero Worship

*I am grateful to those who provided me an example to follow,
but I understand that I must finally follow my own course. I venerate the
saints and sages, but I internalize their lessons and make them my own.
I bow to the true teachers, but I stand on my own two feet.*

If we set some standard against which to judge ourselves, the initial efforts will be pretty frustrating. The conditions that enabled the model or hero to succeed may not exist anymore. The pre-Socratic philosopher, Heraclitus, said, "You can't step into the same river twice." Everything is subject to flux and change—so what worked yesterday may not work today. If we put ourselves into the rigid mold of hero worship, it may work for a time until progress suddenly grinds to a halt. In order to get unstuck, we must jettison the model and forge a new path, which was really the goal in the first place.

One of the yogic realizations is knowing which practices are appropriate to your own time and situation. Reflect for a few minutes on your own spiritual practice. Allow more room in your life for that which works for you. Abandon that which does not work for you. You need not be hasty or rash. Allow the wisdom and insight to come on its own accord.

Social Networks, Not Lone Geniuses

I connect with others who share the same affinities. My work expands as I share with others. I achieve greatness through cooperation, not isolation.

When we think about genius and creativity, we usually think of a lone genius tinkering away in a laboratory until a "Eureka!" moment happens. People love these stories of instant inspiration, like the one about Benjamin Franklin, the kite, and the key—the story of the "discovery" of electricity. The truth is that this old chestnut probably never happened, and certainly Ben Franklin did not discover electricity independently. Probably because of its appealing simplicity, we like the idea of one person (usually male) just having a great idea that changes the world. And yet, as social animals, we do everything in tribes, in packs, in networks, larger than ourselves.

Today, rather than thinking that you must "go it alone," think of the associations or networks that you might join in order to accomplish your goals. Enter into the deep social networks of the world, realizing that the "social" goes beyond even the human world and encompasses any form of connection that one entity might have with another. Picture your consciousness merging with those around you to produce the desired result. Let go of isolation and join the mind of nature.

The Individual and Society

I recognize that the individual and society cannot be separated. I take my place in the community of beings. I welcome others as they welcome me.

My office is located on a row of faculty offices along a hallway at my university in Aiken, South Carolina. It has a gun slit window that cannot be opened, and there is enough space inside to admit the use of a desk, desk chair, computer, three shelves, a filing cabinet, and a single chair for visitors. This space models the monastic cloister, recast for the 1970s in beige institutional styling. If it only had a cot (it does have robes!), the analogy would be complete. And yet our hallway, narrow though it is, also becomes a sort of common room, despite the strictures of its overly efficient design. I cannot recount the number of times that a colleague has saved me from missing a meeting or a grant proposal deadline, because I simply kept my door open (against my sometimes phobic inclinations) to invite the conversation. The cloister has always been a common room; the isolated individual has always been backed by a larger community; the social and the individual are just two sides of the same coin.

Because you are reading this book, you likely have a strong contemplative bent. But do you sometimes miss opportunities because you are so inclined toward introspection? Think of three ways that you can open yourself to other people while maintaining your meditative focus.

The Interface

I recognize humanity as part of the general sociality of all animals. I recognize the contributions of nonhuman nature that make our world livable. I situate myself at the interface between humans and nature.

The interface, the *between*, now marks the site of innovation more than any individual effort or even any one field. Innovation happens when minds get together with nature. This doesn't require beanbag chairs and ping-pong breaks à la dot-com boom Silicon Valley. We need not waste time thinking about ways to rearrange the cubicles so that they will "flow" in a more optimized way. We don't need to inaugurate some more "social" reality, as though that came about with the advent of Facebook. The social nature of humanity *predates humanity*, and it is not likely to go away anytime soon, even if we all become cyborgs.

Today, we attune ourselves to a greater sense of connection that is already in place, recognize the rhythms that permeate all living things, and do not restrict our curiosity to the human sphere. Cultivate here in this silence your natural sense of wonder and curiosity. Allow your mind to roam into the nonhuman, whether it be an artificial intelligence or the behavior of honeybees. Picture yourself joining with the rest of nature, and tear down the artificial walls that divide humanity from nature.

A Quiet Darkness

I set aside my longing for the praise of others. I set aside my longing for power and possessions. I want only to sit in darkness and unfold the mystery of my heart's true desire. I took birth for this moment, for this place and this time.

Why wait any longer? Dwell now in the realization of what you have always wanted to be. Stop looking for external rewards and confirmations. Know your true nature deep inside yourself. Once you have this realization, no one will be able to take it away from you. You may lose sight of it from time to time, but your inner divinity will still be present, glowing like a hot coal on the hearth of the heart. You cause your own sadness by turning away from your innate divinity, by seeking satisfaction from worldly things and the praise of other people. Know the truth for yourself, and you will no longer need the latest fad to make you feel better temporarily.

As you shut your eyes and breathe deeply, the thoughts begin to subside. They become less frantic and insistent. A quiet darkness descends. Rather than run away from that darkness, sit with it. Recognize your troubles as the conjurings of your own mind. Sit there as long as you can. Find the one true desire of your heart, and speak only that into the void. Will yourself to realize your highest vision.

Tenderhearted and Kind

I honor this place and time that I have set aside for meditation.
I honor the divine Self as the heart of my heart.
I welcome all beings in love as I sit in this place.

Little revelations or insights may come after hours of strenuous practice, but they may also come quite easily, as soon as you sit to meditate. When you go to your place of meditation, release the voice of self-criticism that says you haven't worked hard enough, that you don't deserve illumination. Release the voice that brings to mind all of your faults and flaws, that trivializes your dreams and taunts you for having spiritual aspirations. Set aside this sacred space and time, and banish the cruel voices within.

Dear one, withdraw the senses and turn within. Let go of those nagging thoughts. Remember your brothers and sisters throughout the world who long for the same peace and tranquility. Remember the teachers who paved the way for you. As you breathe deeply the inner space opens, and your body becomes light and transparent. You become more welcoming of the world around you. You become very tenderhearted and kind. You await the beauty of everyday life. You return to the world refreshed and alive, eager to love and serve.

A Catalyst for Change

I yield myself to the insight that this quiet time may hold.
I am willing to change my ways of thinking, feeling, and acting in order to
find a more peaceful way of life.

They call it "practice," because mindfulness meditation is difficult and cannot be learned once and for all. The practice makes us stretch our previous limits and grow more deeply in our awareness of the present moment. Mindfulness does not just amount to a coping mechanism, a way to adjust to the stresses of modern life. Mindfulness can be transformative if we will let it affect our life choices. It helps us to see how to make a better way for ourselves and others.

Today, be open to the possibility that you can live in a new way. If you could choose to do something different with your life, big or small, what would it be? Commit now to making three small changes in your life, and visualize them unfolding. As soon as you leave your meditation space, put your vision into practice. Do not delay for even a few minutes.

Just for This, Only This

I set aside my desire for quick results and brilliant visions.
I come to this place only to be here in this place.

I was once at a conference when a participant said, "I have been meditating every day for twenty years, and nothing has really happened." I was impressed with his honesty, but I also thought that maybe he didn't have the full picture. This gentleman was a classical musician and a professor. He earned a decent living at a satisfying job. He was kind, sociable, and knowledgeable. Meditation hadn't taught him to levitate or make fireballs shoot out of his hands, but it had worn away the rough edges, like a stream makes the stones smooth. He had become a good and decent human being, and that is the best that we should want for ourselves.

Today you may find yourself looking for grand results. You might crave ecstatic visions or trance-like states. Just say to yourself, "Whatever happens, I am content," or, "I came here just for this, only this." Then return to the silence or whatever arises for you. Know that a deep inner change is happening even if it doesn't seem flashy or profound.

Indulge Your Curiosity

I honor the questions that have brought me to this hour.
I honor my curiosity as a manifestation of the divine.
I allow my curiosity to take me to true knowledge.

Every religious tradition has miracle stories, whether we are talking about Taoism or Buddhism, Christianity or Islam. These stories, when used appropriately, are meant to be inspiring, to get us to engage with the practices wholeheartedly. These stories are misused when they make us feel small and unworthy, when they are used to remind us of our failings. Be wary of religious figures who use sacred texts in a demeaning manner. You should feel safe and encouraged to question concepts or laugh at a passage that strikes you as funny. A person with true spirituality will be able to answer questions without feeling threatened.

If a question of a religious or philosophical nature arises for you today, do not shove it back into the recesses of your mind. Bring that question to the forefront. See if you can find a satisfactory answer for yourself. Allow the question to lead you to other questions. Indulge your curiosity, and let your curiosity lead to true knowledge.

Connection with Intuition

I set aside information and entertainment.
I reconnect with my intuitive self, with the deeper dimensions of human life.

We live in an age that values information for the sake of information, even when that information can be misleading or false. We live in a world of constant updates and perpetual connection. Little attention gets paid to what is lost in this informational regime. We lose a connection to the intuitive, contemplative side of human existence. Real-world relationships suffer due to technological distractions. Intergenerational knowledge falls by the wayside in the five-minute news cycle. We know more about celebrities we have never even met than we do about our own relatives and next-door neighbors.

We must work hard to recover the connection to the intuitive side of life. This happens when we purposefully disconnect from media, for at least part of the day. Today silence your smartphone and turn off the alerts on your computer. Pay deep attention to your own mind and heart. If you must interact with the written word, let it be something that you write with your own hands, on your computer, or, better yet, on a sheet of blank paper.

Organic Self-Expression

I release the need to express myself through the acquisition of things.
I cultivate my own creative nature organically, and I let go of commercial brands.

Consumer cultures do not do moderation very well. In a consumer culture, moderation or, God forbid, asceticism, can only be viewed as a form of death. In a consumer culture, to buy things and display them is an expression of identity. Not to consume is to be no one. These societies, now devouring the world, cannot stand still even for a moment. The most heretical thing one can do in such a culture is to express oneself organically, without a branded identity.

Entering a higher state of consciousness can be as simple as breathing more deeply over an extended period of time. Today try some deep breathing, adding some music if it helps. Preferably this should be music without a lot of lyrics. When you feel yourself beginning to let go of ordinary awareness, you may work on a specific problem through artwork or musical composition. Go ahead and express your creative self, even if it makes you uncomfortable. You may find a hidden guide there in the creative space, waiting to guide you into a more peaceful way of life.

The Possibility of Change

I embrace my own power as an agent of change.
I allow my doubts to pass away and take concrete action in the world.

Mindfulness does not have to mean passively going through life or taking an apolitical stance. Mindfulness does not have to mean isolation and disconnection. In truth, mindfulness awakens us to the suffering of our fellow human beings and nonhuman life, and may lead to increased engagement with world affairs. As we shake off the false self, with its blithe cynicism, we awaken to the possibility of transformation, for ourselves and for the planet. As the excuses fall away and the fear falls away, we become more willing to put ourselves on the line for others. We embrace risk as a necessary part of life and speak truth to power more confidently.

Allow yourself to think, for just a few minutes, that you really can change the world. You will almost immediately feel wave after wave of internal resistance to this idea. Hold fast to the possibility of change no matter what doubts come your way. See your own power and embrace it. Commit yourself to taking a few small action steps today.

Powers of Observation

I allow my mind to merge with the world around me.
I put all of my effort into observing the world with all of my senses.

Walking in nature sharpens powers of observation. I see a snowy egret launch aloft from a pond, anhingas perched, wings spread, perfectly still, in fallen branches. The trees are mirrored perfectly in the still, gray pond. A slight drizzle falls, and the brown grasses rustle slightly. I hear the clacking of a bicycle chain as a rider passes. The sun hides, a brighter spot in the clouds. Dandelions bloom out of season among the landscaped pansies.

Go for a walk outside today, preferably someplace you find inspiring. Notice as many small things as possible. Pour all of your attention into observation, avoiding the tendency to label and define. Above all, do not allow yourself to think about work, home, or your to-do list. You may wish to write about the experience later, but this is not a necessary part of the exercise.

Giving Freely of Time and Money

I give of my time and money in order to accomplish transformation in the world. If I recognize a course of action as worthwhile and necessary, I will commit the necessary resources to see the job through to completion.

Nothing can ever be accomplished without a ready commitment of resources. This commitment of resources can be outsourced to another person or a corporation, but it cannot be avoided altogether if a creative task is to move forward. Both time and money are necessary in the life of any would-be cultural revolutionary. Good creative outcomes cannot be bought, for money without time leads to undeserved success. Time spent on a task without money to back it up, however, perhaps leads to private fulfillment but does not transform society. Creative spiritual practitioners give of the time and money that they have to put their ideas to work in the world.

As you sit in silence, put your full mind and heart into living from a place of deep commitment. Release that part of your personality that takes shortcuts and implements half measures. Free yourself to realize your dreams completely, holding nothing in reserve. Place fear and doubt in abeyance, and allow your deepest vision to unfold in your life.

Out of the Shallow End

I free myself to realize my full potential. I let go of the safe place that has confined my existence and venture into the unknown.

When I was a kid learning to swim, I would stick closely to the wall in the shallow end of the pool. My mom would tell me, "It's okay! You can swim out in the deeper water. Let go of the side." I knew how to swim but didn't have the necessary confidence, which would take a few more summers. As full-grown adults, we spend much of our lives in this way, having skills and abilities but being afraid to use them. Or we hold back timidly, exercising only a fraction of our talents, afraid of what might happen if we venture into deeper waters.

Perhaps you find yourself today living in an overly cautious manner, afraid to exercise your full potential. See yourself putting all of your ability into what you do. See your life expanding into new areas. Imagine yourself setting aside fear and going into the unknown. Feel deep within yourself that you have the skills that you need to improve your life. Firmly commit yourself to your vision, and venture into the unknown.

Checking the Storehouses

I check over my work from the past to look for half-finished projects. I reuse materials to make the most of my time and resources. Wherever possible, I combine materials to bring plans to fruition.

The creative life necessarily entails a certain excessiveness and results in a messy cutting-room floor of discarded ideas and abandoned projects. Likewise, society casts aside ideas that were ahead of their time or did not fit with the mood of the moment. Because of the natural cycling of time, it makes sense to return to the discard pile and see what can be reworked, what can be put forward under new auspices or new circumstances. Creative spiritual practitioners develop deliberate practices to salvage old projects that have fallen by the wayside, so that maximum efficiency can be put toward a more fulfilling life.

After ten minutes of silent contemplation, look back at your life over the past six to twelve months. You may realize that you have uncompleted projects and plans. See if you can repurpose unused materials, tangible or intellectual, making something out of half-realized potential. This could apply to anything from a home improvement project to a proposal at work to a newfound hobby. If you abandoned your plans for good reason, see if passing the project along to someone else can make the difference.

Working Without Regard for the Results

With regard for my duty, I honor the gods and ancestors. With regard for my duty, I reverence the true teachers. With regard for my duty, I take care of my family. With regard for my duty, I perform my work. With regard for my duty, I serve nonhuman life.

New pursuits often fail, because the desired result did not materialize soon enough or the faltering early efforts met with derision. The spirituality of the Hindu scripture Bhagavad Gita therefore recommends a different path, one in which external rewards do not matter. The person who sees clearly can avoid the "carrot and stick" approach to motivation and focus on the task itself, creating a loophole in which any plan can prosper. Creative spiritual practitioners write themselves a "blank check" in terms of time and effort and put no limits beforehand on what can be achieved. Such practitioners no longer need external rewards or punishments for motivation.

As you look upon your inner landscape today, you may see many impulsive thoughts and trivial desires. You can maintain the meditative state at all times by acting out of concern for duty alone. Concentrate now on what lies within the limits of duty: concentrate on duty and free yourself.

Inner and Outer Alchemy

I cultivate peace in my own mind and heart,
but I also take practical action to make the world a better place.
As I work to transform myself, I also work to transform society.

There are really two aspects to the spiritual life. The first part is the inner alchemy, the endeavor to transmute the base metals of fear and anger into the more refined elements of love and goodwill. The second part is the outer alchemy, the struggle to make the world more just for all beings, not only people but also for nonhuman animals and even inanimate nature. These two aspects are intrinsically linked: we have to do both at the same time. As we engage ourselves in this struggle and join with like-minded individuals, both personal and societal transformation take place.

As you sit in your meditation space today, you may feel incredibly small and powerless. Take a look at your life in your mind's eye. Zoom out so that you see how your life interacts with those around you. Zoom out even further so that you see your place in human society. Zoom out even further so that you see your place in the cycles of nature. Keep going until you see your place in the cosmos. When you are ready, go back down to the individual level: look for any change in emphasis after doing this exercise.

Midday Pause

I give my dreams room to breathe.

Looking out the window at the tree branches swaying in the wind, stopping to look at ants on the sidewalk—these are not diversions from life, but life itself. Let people think you are a little flighty, a little off—who cares?! It is much better to be perceived as eccentric than to be ground into bits by relentless demands. A life without revery, without daydreams, without magic, isn't really worth living. Better to keep your head in the clouds than in the sand.

As you enter your practice space today, you may feel a little guilty for taking this pause. Notice that feeling of guilt or shame that says you have more productive things to be doing. Acknowledge this feeling, but don't let it rule you. Placate this guilt-mongering voice by telling it that you will be able to work much better after a brief rest. Sit here in the quiet and allow yourself to recharge.

Defeating the Inner Enemy

I behold the inner light, which teaches me stillness rather than busyness, contentment rather than desire, creativity rather than conformity.

The inner enemy alone keeps us from true illumination. This inner enemy, the ego nature or the self, leads to the path of least resistance, the easy way that sacrifices the goal in favor of easy pleasures. The inner enemy also attributes blame to other people when we fail to realize the goal, getting us to conform to what we *think* other people want from us. In order to achieve freedom or liberation, we have to hold fast to the inner light rather than looking toward the ego and its schemes.

As you close your eyes to meditate, picture a radiant light in the chest region, which slowly expands to become a sphere much larger than your own body, which becomes porous and transparent. The light encompasses and envelops you. It is all-sufficient for your every need. As distractions arise, allow them to fade before the all-encompassing light. The light frees from every bond.

Dealing with Social Anxiety

I give myself the permission to make mistakes in interacting with other people. I will try to be empathetic, but I know that I sometimes misunderstand. I live into the fullness of my humanity and make peace with my awkwardness.

No matter how strong your empathic ability, you will still sometimes read the cues wrong and offend someone or intrude on someone else's space. The fear of offending, the fear of getting it wrong can be paralyzing. Sometimes this fear can develop into full-scale social anxiety, to the point where it is easier to be alone than to have to worry about the feelings of other people. Social anxiety fades when we give ourselves the freedom to make mistakes, when we acknowledge that we will not always be able to please other people but we know our intentions are good. In the absence of a perfect reading of the social situation, we just have to do the best that we can.

Perhaps today you struggle with having to go into a crowd or speaking before an audience. Breathe deeply into your fear and discomfort. Breathe into your nervous stomach. Breathe into the tightening in your chest. Breathe into the lump in your throat. Breathe into the tension in your head. Keep the breath circulating. Allow the chest cavity to expand as you deepen and lengthen the breath. Invite calm and tranquility into your life. When you are ready, take this calm with you into the realm of social interaction.

Gray Days and Gloomy Moods

When I am feeling sad and downhearted, I recognize these emotions and sit with them. I do not need to be superhuman. I just keep going, despite my despair.

Some days it can be hard to get out of bed. Sometimes work seems dull and meaningless. Sometimes everything seems bleak and lifeless, either in the world at large or in our own personal sphere. During such times, you do not have to force yourself to be more cheerful or optimistic. It can sometimes be more useful to sit with the distressing thoughts and acknowledge them. It's okay to just sit there and say, yes, I'm feeling a bit hopeless today. Sometimes just sitting with these thoughts can diffuse them more than wrestling with or ignoring them.

Perhaps today you are feeling sad and gloomy. Look into your own inner disposition and get into contact with your negative feelings. Draw very close to these negative thoughts and sensations, and try to be very detailed in your observations. You can do this without doing a lot of mental description: just feel very deeply. When you return to your ordinary routine, simply recognize and accept the gloom. You don't need to muscle through it: merely welcome the gloominess as an odd sort of companion, neither desirable nor undesirable, neither true nor false.

Fuel for the Fire

I release the need to solve problems, to be effective, to do things, to accomplish and be accomplished. My thoughts and feelings wind down, slowly, and stop. I allow myself to stop.

The dead stalks of rabbit tobacco amongst the dried stalks of corn become fuel for the fall burnover. The field, cut clean, lies fallow for the winter. The burning makes way for spring. And the green shoots will rise from these furrows soon. The dirt awaits the plow. And sits and waits. But the lying fallow must happen. The field must wait.

As you sit here in the silence, allow your body, your heart, and your mind to lie still and open. When the mental disturbances come, offer them as fuel for the fire. Let yourself become a field, shorn down to the earth, all of the weeds burned. Sit still and wait. Do nothing.

Making the Passage of Time Work for You

I concentrate with one-pointed attention, putting my whole effort into the things that I do. I work in a concentrated manner, every day, to achieve my goals.

In the Hindu goddess—based prayer called the *Devi Mahatmyam*, one of the demons is named "Want of Resolution," and another demon is called "Wandering To and Fro." The mother goddess, called Chandi, the destroyer of thoughts, slays the demons with the pike of concentration and the discus of revolving time. In other words, careless efforts fail to produce the desired fruits, which can only be brought into existence through disciplined, concentrated effort over time. The sharpness of the pike, the weapon of divinity, is directly related to the sharpness of concentration that we bring into our lives through systematic effort. Time works in favor of disciplined action but against erratic action.

Today, choose whether time will bring your efforts to fruition or devour your efforts through entropy. Sit with concentrated attention, fixing the mind on the point between the brows, controlling the breath. Make your back as straight as you can. When you leave the meditation space, put the same kind of attention into your work.

The Rarest Commodity

I look to silence as my chief guide and counsel. I use the silence to know myself, and, in knowing myself, I find freedom.

The most costly and rare commodity of our time is not gold or platinum or diamonds. The most costly commodity in the world today is silence, so rare as to be almost completely absent from our lives. Silence is the best teacher of all. Silence makes us see, in stark clarity, our preoccupations and beliefs, our fears and obsessions. And, if we can hold to silence long enough, it provides not only the diagnosis but also the cure. The person who can sit in silence without agitation can do anything without agitation.

Today, get to the most quiet environment that you can muster for meditation. If your space is not completely quiet, that is fine. Focus instead on quieting the mind. Or listen to the little background noises, like distant traffic or the shushing sound of fans and air conditioning. Hold everything back except these little sounds. Embrace the silence, and let it teach you.

Unleashing the Inner Dweeb

I allow myself to love what I love. I allow myself to love who I love. I give myself permission to do what makes me joyful, even if others do not understand.

As school children we learn the unofficial curriculum of blending in with the crowd. We don't want to be labeled as dorks or dweebs, nerds or imbeciles. So we learn to alter our personalities a bit, to tamp down the weirdness and originality. Unfortunately, this habit persists into adulthood, and life loses some of its shine as we push ourselves into this personality that doesn't quite fit. But, as we age, we can begin to recover the suppressed dork, to find those weird things that make life worth living. Maybe that one nerdy something goes from being a side concern to being a reason for living.

Have you dropped one of your hobbies or interests because you thought it wasn't cool enough? As you sit in your meditation space today, you may notice social pressures intruding on your thought processes. You may notice this subtle tailoring to imagined expectations. Release the thoughts of these expectations, one by one. Imagine yourself to be free and unencumbered. Reduce the inner censorship of your personality.

Fear of Missing Out

I release my need for constant updates through electronic media.
I set aside time to interact with the people around me.

Movie theaters now have a reminder before the feature that says, *Please remember to silence your electronic devices*. Easier said than done. Technology only gets more obtrusive as the years go by, so that it becomes difficult not to look at a tiny screen or a big screen every five minutes. The fear of missing out (FOMO) is reported as a major reason why young people, especially, cannot get away from social media. But fear of missing out goes both ways. By tuning in to technology, we lose face-to-face encounters and interactions with the natural world. We should have some time, even a few minutes, set aside each day when electronics are not invited.

Today, resolve to take a few minutes or a few hours without checking email, text messages, or social media. When you feel the itch to pick up a device, remind yourself of the good things in your life that do not exist in electronic form. Take the time to talk to one of your loved ones, go for a walk in nature, or pick up a pen and paper.

Not Getting It Right

I release myself from the need to have it all together. I release myself from the desire for a perfect life. I release myself from my own judgments, and I release myself from the judgments of others.

We spend most of our lives running away from something or running toward something. We try to accomplish our educational and career goals. We try to have the perfect relationships, the perfect family life. We desperately want to avoid the judgments of others, the perception that all is not well, that we do not *have it together*. This management of perceptions gets so exhausting, and yet continue it must. We can't just drop out of society, so we play the game. And yet meditation and mindfulness provide the slightest loophole, an invisible place of refuge. Maybe we cannot drop everything and go live in a cave, but we can withdraw into the cave of the heart, this invisible place of stillness that we carry with us all the time.

Here, in this silent place, there is no *getting it right*, no *doing it right*. Allow yourself to just be here, with all of your faults and flaws intact. Everything that is wrong with you is also what is right with you. All of your imperfections are also your perfections. From the highest vantage point, there is not one single thing wrong in the whole universe. It is okay to just stop here for a moment, to allow yourself to just be.

One Point of View among Many

I acknowledge that I do not have a complete understanding
of my own life or my contributions to society.
Lacking complete knowledge, I have mercy on myself for my own failings.
I admit the blind spots in my vision and open myself to insight.

Keep in mind that your perspective on your life is just that—one perspective among many possible perspectives. You may not be able to see your own contributions to your workplace or your family clearly. Sometimes other people may be able to judge your gifts more accurately. Especially bring the partiality of your own vision to mind when you are castigating yourself for not working hard enough, for not earning enough money, or any other perceived shortfall. You simply don't have the full picture. Chances are that you make a much larger difference in your world than you think.

Today you may find yourself in the mode of self-criticism, reciting a litany of things that you have done wrong or tasks that you have not completed. Allow yourself to see the partiality of your own point of view, the blind spots in your self-knowledge. Move from a place of self-judgment and self-condemnation to a place of agnosticism about your own motivations. Make room for insights, but don't try to force them into place.

How to Feel Less Overwhelmed

I do not need to get everything done today;
I just need to make some progress. I can take care of myself and my
responsibilities today. My good is compatible with the good of
those around me. My good is compatible with the good of the world.

As you think about all of the things that you need to do today, you may quickly feel overwhelmed. You have the various areas of your job responsibility, errands to run, chores to be done, and you still want to take care of healthy eating and your exercise regimen. Keep in mind that today is only one day. You don't need to do everything today, so long as you do something to contribute positively to each *area* of concern in your life. You just have to touch all of the bases, so to speak, which is different from accomplishing every item on your to-do list. Each day should have some attention to work, to home and family, and to self-care.

As you breathe deeply into your heart center, breathe blessings into your work. Then breathe blessings into your home and family life. Then breathe blessings into your physical and emotional health. Finally, breathe blessings into all the people in the world. Then breathe blessings into all plant and animal life. Wish for the good of all beings.

Living on Purpose

I work in a coordinated fashion to make my dreams a reality. As I plan my priorities, I feel more relaxed with my progress going forward. I move steadily and inexorably toward my deepest vision.

When I was an elementary school student, I was the one with the messy desk, untied shoes, and an untucked shirt. I was smart but disorganized. In fact, I had a deep suspicion of time management and planning going right into my young adulthood. I associated advance preparation with being "anal retentive" or having a "type A personality." I now see the benefit of working on things in advance, even though I still sometimes have trouble with structure and hierarchy. I have come to realize that a little bit of planning goes a long way, that even imperfect organization goes a long way toward feeling more at ease.

Take this time of meditation to reflect on your true goals in life. Allow your inner guide, your muse or guardian angel, to speak to you during this time of quiet. It may help to light a candle or listen to some devotional music. Open your heart and mind to insight. When you have completed your allotted time of meditation, make a concrete plan to realize your dreams.

Do Not Settle

I give myself the reward of my own best effort.
I give myself the reward of living according to my highest vision.
I give myself the reward of strong work and good relationships.

So often we settle for less than our best in life. We may think that, in so doing, we are *sticking it to the man*, but we really only cheat ourselves. Each of us deserves to have stimulating relationships, rewarding careers, bounteous well-being, and a sound emotional life. When one of these elements gets out of whack, we tend to either blame other people or hate ourselves. The blame game only makes the situation worse, as we channel our efforts into recriminations. It would be much better to identify problems before they get worse and then take concrete action steps, even if those action steps only help us meander in the right direction.

As you look within your heart today, you may see traces of the blaming mindset. You may blame an employer, a spouse, or yourself for unhappiness in life. You may be retaining perceived wrongs from the past for your misfortune. Allow yourself to release these negative memories and emotions. Allow yourself a fresh start. Open your heart and mind to new possibilities, more bold and beautiful than you have previously imagined.

Positive Change out of Crisis

I acknowledge my deep hurt over the failings of the past, but I do not let my feelings bind me. I await a new direction and make the leap into the unknown when the time comes.

As a younger person I had a goal in life of serving as a Protestant minister, which I viewed as a true calling. When I actually spent time in the church, though, I found it to be intellectually and emotionally stifling. I experienced leaving the church as a profound personal failure and a major life crisis, but it led me to my career in academia and my eventual discovery of Indian philosophy and religion. A rather unfortunate situation gave me a new beginning, one that opened new horizons of meaning and fulfillment in my life. In retrospect I am glad that I did not force myself down a path that was not a good fit for me.

Perhaps you have had crises and failures in your own life. You may find yourself clinging to the old way rather than making the leap into something new. Allow yourself a few minutes to let go of the past. You may not yet understand the new direction that you need to take. Sit here for a few minutes, not knowing what to do next. Set your mind and heart in patient awaiting for a new direction.

Welcoming Strangers

I do not arrogantly stand above the strangers in the land.
I practice hospitality to those who cross my path.

As of this writing, refugees are making their way out of Northern Africa and the Middle East and into Europe and other parts of the world, at considerable danger. They cross the rough seas or journey over thousands of miles by land, risking their lives for the promise of a better life than they had in the war-torn lands they left behind. Rather than labeling such people as criminals or terrorists, the world should support these courageous individuals in any way possible and work to make them a part of our societies. Treating refugees with dignity and respect, to include extending full citizenship, is a moral duty and not a special favor.

Look deep within your heart center and find the radiant warmth of a thousand suns that leads you to respect and welcome the stranger and the outcast. Sit here and cultivate that open-hearted feeling until it becomes strong and enduring. At the end of your allotted period of meditation, make a list of a few things that you can do to improve the lot of the refugees among us.

Struggle Is Greater Than Resignation

I may not be able to practice perfectly, but I continue to meditate and work on my life. Even when circumstances do not favor me, I continue to meditate and work on my life. Even when my spirit lags, I continue to meditate and work on my life.

It is not uncommon to feel inadequate or even hypocritical when doing meditative work. As I look at my life, I see my less-than-perfect diet and my sloppy exercise regimen. I see how after so many years of spiritual practice, I still find my meditation interrupted by thoughts about what I am going to eat for lunch. But I believe that I will be a better person if I do the practice, and so I continue. I won't let the perfect become the enemy of the good, and so I keep trying. We should all keep trying, as struggle is greater than resignation.

As you look at your own mental landscape, do you see places where you have resigned yourself to failure? If your life were a garden, and your practice the fence around that garden, would there be places where the fence has fallen down? Feel the attitude of resignation and replace it with struggle. Build your willpower to continue the practice even when you feel like quitting. Feel the bliss that awaits those who persevere in the practice.

Natural Abundance

I do not depend on my own efforts but allow for inspiration to arise naturally. I make myself available to the work, but I do not try to force it. I feel a natural abundance of ideas, a natural abundance of time, and a natural abundance of resources.

Sometimes inspiration doesn't go in a straight line. If you feel stuck on one project, switch to another job that gets you more excited. Just be sure that you are not practicing avoidance. If you are genuinely trying to make progress on a task, and it just isn't working, try doing something else. Also check the state of your physical body. You may need to rest, eat something, or get some exercise. When you come back to your work, you may find that it flows better.

As you take this midday break, be gentle with your own mind and body. Don't try to force yourself into relaxing. Just notice whatever occurs before consciousness. Notice any sensations that come into your body. Breathe deeply, and pay attention to the breath. Allow the peaceful and abundant state to arise naturally. Just be open to the experience.

Rest and Contemplation

*I give myself this midday pause so that I can recharge
and take the time to appreciate life. I can see more clearly
when I give my mind a break in the middle of the day.*

A chef knows when to stir the pot and when to let it simmer. A novelist knows how to withhold information to build suspense. A composer knows that rests can introduce tension and interest into music. Our societies need to learn more about pauses and silences, for they really make life come together. Life can be so much more beautiful and significant when we take the time to appreciate it, a little bit at a time, each day.

As you sit here during this midday moment of rest and contemplation, you may be feeling tired. You may feel frustrated that you have not been able to accomplish more. Give yourself a break for the time being. Everything will come to fruition in due time. Rest your mind and rest your eyes. Fill your heart with gratitude for the gift of this day.

Day by Day

*I set into motion today the habit of mindfulness that
will follow me wherever I go. I set aside this place and time
as sacred so that every place and time might become sacred.*

You shower every day and brush your teeth twice a day. You eat and drink every day and check your email every day. Why should it be so difficult to spend some time in meditation every day? Each day's practice builds on the momentum that was formed the day before. Eventually, meditation, whether we are talking about mantra practice, ritual worship, or silent meditation, becomes an ingrained habit. It gradually becomes less difficult to sit down and enter that reflective frame of mind. Maybe you haven't reached that point yet, but you will soon. And, if you lose the habit, it is easy to go right back again.

As you sit today, bind your power of will to this present moment. Forge a new link in the chain of habit that keeps you engaged in awareness. Feel your powers of attention growing stronger today. Listen deeply to whatever this moment holds for you. Picture the habit of mindfulness growing stronger and stronger, day by day.

Beyond Human Divisions

I set aside my conditioning and become one with the mass of humanity yearning for a better way of life. I open my heart and mind for the practice of peace.

Meditation and mindfulness tend to dissolve ties of nationality and ethnicity. The great yogis, like Shirdi Sai Baba and Shri Ramakrishna, welcomed people of all nationalities and religions, of all castes and income levels. They transcended geography and ideology and became a refuge for all who came to them. In the space of meditation we truly become one in our desire for peace and harmony, in our yearning for a better way of life. The transcendental consciousness that we glimpse in meditation suspends normal time and space, so that we see and experience the underlying reality beyond human divisions.

As you survey your mental landscape, take note of any prejudice that may stand in the way of ultimate realization. Surrender any claim to superiority based on personal income, nationality, ethnicity, or education. Mentally bow in respect before every other creature. Take a silent vow to share every single insight that you gain in meditation for the good of all.

Crowds and Contentment

I find peace and tranquility today, whether I am alone or with other people.

You may think of yourself as either an extrovert or an introvert, but take these conclusions with a grain of salt. We can easily typecast ourselves into personality traits that may be the case some of the time but do not really amount to permanent features of our identities. Sometimes a day spent conducting a lot of business among people passes quickly and easily, and sometimes being alone can be delightful. Mindfulness practice helps us to accept the situation, whether we find ourselves in solitude, in a crowd, or some combination of the two.

Now that you find yourself with a few minutes to spare, picture in your mind's eye the invisible connections that bind you to the people in your world, whether in real life or virtual space. See the vast web of connections circling the globe, and picture those connections enfolded with love, peace, and goodwill. Strive to carry these benevolent feelings with you today, whether you are alone or among other people.

Confidence and Courage

I abandon half efforts and take concrete action to solve the problems in my life that bother me the most. I have all of the willpower, resources, and ability that I need to change things for the better.

The problems that plague our lives may seem immutable, but they can ultimately be transcended, for everything that we know as real continually changes. We may have long-standing, seemingly intractable problems with health, money, and relationships, but we can always choose a new course of action. People can and do recover from poor finances, chronic illnesses, and abusive relationships; it just takes the power of effort combined with supportive community and expert guidance. We must commit ourselves and take concrete actions—abandoning half measures and halfheartedness—to improve the conditions in our lives.

As you look at the long-standing problems in your life, you may feel your confidence waning and your mood deflating. Breathe into your heart center and picture your stores of confidence and courage rising, as though you have a large sphere of energy radiating from the chest. Know yourself to be completely empowered, with all of the support that you need to overcome your troubles. Do not move from the meditation space until you are positively excited about taking control of the situation that bothers you most.

Sharing Inspiration

As I find my own inspiration,
I become an inspiration for others.

As you have become more habituated to the process of mindfulness and meditation, you begin to sense changes in your mood and outlook. You have a little more spring in your step as you let go of the continual complaining that characterized your old life. People begin to notice your increased optimism and higher energy levels. Perhaps you can gently and unobtrusively share your secret. Perhaps you can start a meditation group where you live or work. As you share with others and inspire them, your own joy increases.

Now that you have reached the middle of your day, think of how your life connects with the people around you. Cultivate an inner attitude of joy and abundance. Let go of any frustrations and worries that may have accumulated over the course of this day. See yourself becoming an inspiration for others.

Transforming the Ordinary

I keep active and alert, taking note of any changes within my environment. Rather than resisting change, I look for hidden opportunities.

Today you may be feeling a little ho-hum, like you have been stuck doing the same thing for years. Take a closer look: there is always something new to be discovered. Maybe you have a new coworker down the hall, or maybe a new initiative has come down from management. Maybe a new restaurant has just opened down the street you can try. Rather than going with that knee-jerk resistance to change, see if you can make something positive of it. You may discover a new bright spot in your life rather than just a bore or a chore.

Because change is the very nature of the temporal universe, nothing ever stands still. As you close your eyes for meditation, take a look at the processes in your own body. As you make yourself very calm and still, you can hear and feel your breath going in and out, the *lub-dub* of the heart muscle, and the tiny sensations of the circulation of blood.

Destroying Inadequacy

I am inspired, capable, and fortunate. I bring the best of my considerable abilities into everything that I do, and I reap the benefits of an abundant life.

Most people suffer from a hidden inferiority complex. Everyone walks around all day, feeling incapable, unattractive, and unlucky, without ever knowing that the people around them feel the same way. If these thoughts and feelings were really true, the earth would have stopped turning on its axis a long time ago. These self-critical feelings have little basis in reality, but they act as a hidden governor, keeping us held into predetermined pathways of action. For the really big transformations to occur, we have to entirely disregard and destroy feelings of inadequacy and demand the very best that life has to offer. This transformation can only occur from the inside out, by feeling worthy and then acting in accordance with that worthiness.

Today, see if you can identify some of the sob stories that you tell yourself about your life. Name these falsehoods one by one as they arise in your mind's eye. Simply say the word "false" and pass on to the next sob story. Keep going until your frame of mind is calm.

Maintaining Consistency in the Midst of Change

I do not wait for ideal circumstances or favorable conditions. I find myself here, in this present, whatever may happen or not happen.

We have an inbuilt bias for the comfortable and familiar, for the business-as-usual scenario. We usually think that things will continue to be the way they have always been. Note that this can be true only in a local or regional sense, and only within narrow time horizons and specific parameters. Big upheavals occur all the time, and we need to position ourselves to take advantage of them. Meditation allows us to increase our powers of observation so that we can respond in a more agile way to change as it occurs.

As you look back over the last week or two, were you thrown off-balance by a chance event? Were you caught flat-footed because you expected your old, familiar routine? Today, cultivate alertness. Sit on the edge of your seat, as though everything could change at any moment. Attune yourself to the razor's edge of the unfolding present. Become light and nimble, ready to adapt at a moment's notice.

Dealing with Naysayers

I continue in the practice for my own benefit, no matter what anyone else says or does. I will not allow myself to be derailed by skeptical doubts.

You may have someone in your life who nay-says your meditative practice. They may tell you, "I read this article that says meditation has no effect." Or maybe they *accidentally* interrupt you every time you sit. Or they may espouse a life philosophy completely opposite to your own. In such situations it is okay to set boundaries by saying, "I realize that you don't believe in this practice, but it is important to me." If they continue to bother you, feel free to limit the scope of the relationship or minimize your encounters with the intrusive person. Or you may choose to change your timing, so that the subject does not arise.

As you sit quietly in your meditation space, picture in your mind's eye the person who most often derails your practice. Cultivate compassion for that person, knowing that some deep disappointment or pain likely lies behind their skeptical doubts. You may not be able to change that person's behavior, but be open to the possibility of change in the relationship at some other time, in some other situation.

Stay with the Moment

I acknowledge that enlightenment belongs to everyone
and not to a select few. I choose enlightenment for myself.
I stay present in this moment for this time of contemplation.

Enlightenment, the process of clarifying the mind, belongs to all human beings and not a select few. We have monastics and holy people so that ordinary householders might be inspired to undertake the practices that lead to illumination. That said, for both monastics and laypeople, a certain amount of effort must be exerted in order to bring the mind into a more peaceful state. Otherwise we get trapped in cycles of greed and anger without even realizing it. The work of liberation can never be completed once and for all. Even great saints had to keep practicing after receiving their highest visions.

As you sit in your meditation space today, focus on being fully present to this moment. Imagine that the past and future do not exist. Stay with the work of liberation for these few minutes of calm. This time that you spend here will be the most important part of the day. Stay with the moment.

Clearing the Dust

I recognize my need to clear away mental debris.
I emerge from my practice with a sharp and clear mind,
seeing things as they are rather than how I would like them to be.

Common household dust contains tiny particles of fibers and mold, human and pet hair, little bits of skin, sand and pollen, and even debris from outer space! It collects whether we like it or not, rain or shine, 365 days a year. So we have to sweep, mop, and dust our floors and furniture. In the same way, our minds collect the detritus of half-formed fragments of dreams and memories, snippets of music and visual images. We clean the mind through mindfulness and meditation, so that we can see and understand more clearly.

As you sit down to meditate, your mind may be racing ahead to the things still left to do. To calm the busy mind, root yourself in place, feeling the sit bones connecting with the floor, cushion, or chair. Feel gravity pulling down on you, and keep your spine as straight as you are able. As you breathe deeply, feel the many thoughts (dust) dissipating. Become simultaneous with yourself: no running ahead in anticipation or looking backward in memory.

Afraid of the Dark

I may be afraid of what I will find in meditation, but I confidently go into the inner darkness. I allow myself to be reborn in stillness.

There will always be something else to do or say, something to occupy our time and attention. Entertainment is only a click away for most of us. This space of meditation is something different, and it can be a bit scary. We are afraid of what we might find there in the dark and quiet. We are desperately afraid of being bored, of having to keep still, and of what we might learn about ourselves. The only way to get over our fear of the dark is to plunge into it.

You may think of the internal space as a vast emptiness, as a dark cellar, or as an expanse of white light. Its unknown, undefined quality can be jarring. If you find yourself wanting to recoil from the inner space, come back to the breath. Move your breath energy (prana) up the spinal column, creating a current of energy that goes up the spine and through the crown of your head.

Cravings and Sleep

I look behind my cravings to the feelings that motivate them. I carefully observe any negative feelings and confront them directly.

At midday, you may be feeling powerful cravings, for caffeine, for chocolate, for french fries, for sex. Before you indulge, take a look at what might be lying behind the craving. You may see boredom, sadness, hopelessness, or frustration. Sit with these feelings and notice them in detail. Attend to the emotions and the bodily sensations that accompany them. Even make them more intense if you like. Really paying attention to these feelings can diffuse them.

As you pay attention to the craving, you may find yourself just on the boundary of sleep, especially if you are operating on a sleep deficit. See if you can play with this borderland, bringing yourself back and forth between attention and drowsiness. You may receive a helpful vision or insight in this zone between napping and wakefulness. Try to avoid falling into deep sleep, but you needn't fear this gray area.

Fear: Friend and Foe

I welcome fear as an indicator of risk, which makes life worth living. I face my fear, taking decisive action whenever necessary. As I move toward my fear, my life changes for the better.

A life lived without fear is a life lived without risk. Without fear, life would be pretty dull. At the same time, no one can be afraid all the time, because that also makes for a terrible existence. At its best, fear indicates that we have moved to the very edge of familiarity and into a place of risk, small or large. Where there is no fear, there is likely avoidance of some painful situation that really needs to be addressed.

Pay attention to any feelings of fear that you have now. Are you fearful of overdrafting your bank account? Of a presentation you have to give? Of an uncomfortable conversation that you need to have with a loved one? After sitting here with your fear for a few minutes, go ahead and undertake that action that makes you afraid. Let knowledge overcome fear as you act decisively.

Invisible Wounds

I pay close attention to the wounds that I carry. As I acknowledge my wounds, I allow the healing process to begin.

Little kids love getting Band-Aids, especially if they have famous characters on them, for even the most minor scrape. Of course, it's just a little gauze with an adhesive strip, but to kids the Band-Aid has magical powers of healing. Kids just want the wound *to be recognized*, and, as adults, we need the same thing. As long as we keep trying to pretend that nothing is wrong, our physical and emotional ills only get worse. When we truly attend to our wounds, the healing begins.

Today, try a few minutes of spiritual journaling about some aspect of the past that you have trouble releasing. Write in longhand on some notebook paper, describing the event that has caused you distress. Be as detailed as possible, recalling the scene with as much vividness as you can muster. When you have finished, burn or shred the pages.

Normal and Paranormal

I maintain my normal life as I continue my spiritual practice. I take care of all of my affairs so that all obstacles may be quelled.

Since you are reading this book, chances are pretty good that you believe in one or more occult or supernatural phenomena: astral projection, ESP, remote viewing, telekinesis, and the like. Believing in the paranormal is all well and good, so long as it does not get in the way of exercising our *normal* powers. We should do everything in our power by means of quotidian self-effort, and only then should we turn to consulting our psychic abilities. I have nothing at all against the occult, so long as it doesn't become a form of escape.

As you continue your meditation regimen, take care that you do not neglect your normal life. After sitting in silence for a few minutes, take a long walk or go to the gym. Pay your bills. Take care of anything at work that you have neglected. Remember that you are in this meditation practice for the long haul: arrange your life so that you can continue this practice indefinitely. Do not rob Peter to pay Paul.

Stereotypes about the Creative Life

I leave room for the work that gives me joy. I give myself the space for self-expression while keeping the commitments that I have already made. Joy and duty are not mutually exclusive.

There is a stereotype of creative people, like authors, actors, and musicians, that they must have disastrous personal lives, going through several marriages and drinking heavily, going on serious meds and taking trips through rehab. See if you harbor some stereotypes about what your life would look like if you had maximum productivity. Then imagine, for a few minutes, that you can lead the life of your dreams without giving up family life, without becoming an addict, without divorcing your spouse. Believe in the possibility of living with creativity, with integrity, with fulfillment, all the while keeping the commitments that you have already made.

As you close your eyes in meditation, see all of your areas of life responsibility arrayed before you. Work, home, hobbies, and relationships are displayed before your mind's eye. Picture these parts of your life functioning together harmoniously, completely without conflict of any sort. See the pieces of the puzzle falling into place. Through force of will, picture all conflicts dissolving, all excuses evaporating.

Keep Growing

I allow the best that I have within me to reach its full expression. I allow myself to grow and change with the seasons, until I reach full maturity.

My grandfather Tom would pick up a green pinecone, sit down on the front porch steps, and whittle away the outside with his pocket knife until he got down to the pine nuts. I don't think he ate them; he just took a kind of joy in seeing these seeds inside the spiky green cone. He also wanted to show off for his grandkids, who thought (and still think) that he was pretty much the best thing ever. He was a part-time farmer and kept a greenhouse of tropical houseplants as well as several large fields of vegetables. He taught me of the secret life of fruition in botany, the ever-growing impulse of plants. And if we, as people, can mimic that impulse to keep growing, we will be just fine, no matter what the world throws at us.

As you sit here in meditation, hold a silent intention for all of your potential to reach its full fruition in the world. As places of resistance arise in your mind and heart, release them, resolving to hold nothing back in the quest for the full expression of your spiritual and creative powers. Keep clarity within, allowing only the inner light to shine.

Making the Impossible Manageable

I may not have a lot of time, but I do have some time. I will use my time, even a few minutes, to accomplish my most important goals.

Busy people know how to get things done: in five- or ten-minute increments of time. Think of the biggest, most exciting goal in your life. Then start chipping away at it, a few minutes at a time. At first the task will seem so large as to be impossible, but your efforts will begin to make a small dent and then a bigger dent. Gradually the insurmountable becomes manageable. And then the biggest, most fantastic dream becomes a reality. All because you set aside a few minutes here and there.

As you sit here in silent contemplation, you may have a dream that you have deferred indefinitely. Your heart may be sinking in hurt and disappointment. You may feel resentful that your life does not afford you the time to do what you love. Resolve here in this quiet space to turn your time and attention toward your dream. As soon as you close your time of meditation, take a little bit of time to devote to your most lofty goal.

Steady, Plodding Effort

*I give thanks today for the gift of work that keeps my hands
busy and my mind attentive. I put my whole self into my endeavors,
knowing that one day my reward will come.*

Not every day can be a breakthrough day. Whether we are talking about professional life, creative pursuits, or spiritual disciplines, the vast majority of time will be spent in steady, plodding effort. That said, these ordinary times of mundane effort empower the big breakthroughs. The big flashes of insight do not occur without the time spent searching and reaching. By working today, you stow a hidden cache of gems that one day will be revealed.

As you sit here in quiet contemplation, cultivate a feeling of gratitude for the small, daily efforts in your life. Let go of all feelings of tedium and futility. Know deep within your heart that today's efforts have mattered, that you have spent your time on worthwhile pursuits. If feelings of self-blame or inadequacy arise, release them. Sit here for a few minutes in quiet appreciation.

On Inspiration

My muse comes when I call, giving me an endless supply of ideas with which to ply my chosen craft. As I carry out the inspiration that I receive, I come into greater connection with the source of my well-being.

Inspiration is not a feeling or a voice from heaven. Inspiration is a spirit of willingness, a desire to see a task through to its completion. Inspiration is taking joy in the doing of a thing. Inspiration can carry you aloft, like a magic carpet, but it can also drag you through the mud, like a game of tug-of-war. Inspiration stays with you if you stay with it. If you tell it to go bother someone else, it will do so at a moment's notice. At the same time, if you ask for it, it will come.

If you are feeling uninspired today, look deeply into your heart. Ask your questions there in the stillness of the cave of the heart. But you must not ask for something in exchange for nothing. No, ask to be given a job to do. It can be something small, but inspiration needs materials on which to work. So you must have something to do: on paper, with clay, with a broom or a mop, with a trowel and bricks. Inspiration can work in any medium, but it must have a material basis.

Little by Little

I push past obstacles by degrees, little by little. I keep my mind focused, unwavering, knowing that I will not fail to reach my goal.

Get the door open just a crack, and you can swing it wide. Be faithful in one thing, and you will be given many things. Think about the grass and dandelions that can grow in the tiniest crack in the sidewalk. Think about how the steady dripping of water can gradually carve solid rock in a canyon or build glistening stalactites in a cave. You don't have to accomplish everything today: just make the most of what you have been given.

As you close your eyes in meditation, you may be feeling dissatisfied in one way or another in some part of your life. Invite a spirit of relief into your mind and body to soothe your frayed nerves, your restless heart. Ask for the wisdom to understand the correct action to improve the area of your life that gives you trouble. Ask for an understanding of one thing you need to do to get to the place where you want to be.

Work and Enchantment

I approach this moment with wonder and expectation.
I await the magic of work well-done.

In our seriousness about life, we sometimes suck the joy right out of our work. We are so concerned with output, with productivity, that we forget the magical nature of work. Why not let work become an occasion for meeting the muses? Why not allow for spirits to guide us in our interactions with our machines? Something fantastic happens when we allow for computing to become conjuration, for writing to become wizardry. We can take the best insights of bygone ages and combine them with the best elements of our technological age.

As you sit here in the quiet space of meditation, try to avoid being so serious and stern. You never know what this session will bring. Keep alive the possibility for magic. Maybe the gods will favor you with a visit. Or maybe you will hear the strains of the celestial music. Maybe some new enchantment is just a few breaths away.

Naturally Good

I don't have to fit myself into a predetermined image of goodness. I embrace all parts of my nature, recognizing in myself the divine love.

It can be just as much of a mistake to live too straightlaced as it is to live too recklessly. Erring in either direction leads to a diminishment in the enjoyment of life. Somewhere between the two extremes lies the sweet spot of being slightly roguish but good-natured as well. Maybe you know someone like this, who knows how to have a good time but still manages to be kind and decent. You would want to go to a party with her, but you feel like you could call her if you were in a jam.

Today you might have in your head an ideal version of the person-who-meditates. You check yourself against this ideal and find yourself lacking. Set aside that ideal as you sit here and meditate. Strive to be nothing other than who you are in this moment. You don't have to try to be a good person: you are naturally good, just the way that you are.

Mourning the Loss of the Sacred

I honor and respect the first peoples of the world, their medicines and rituals. I will do whatever I can to preserve sacred places.

In the traditional cultures of the world, sacred places were bound up with certain prayers and incantations, and perhaps dances and ritual gestures, which were also connected to botanicals ingested by the initiate. Gods and spirits were associated with these plants, these places, these songs. Today we have this physicalist bent that says that the chemical compound works regardless of place, regardless of the sacred function. We don't trust anything that has not been patented by a major corporation.

So many peoples and languages of the world have been lost due to Western consumer civilization. So many plant and animal species as well. Take a few minutes now to mourn this loss. Silently vow to save what can be saved and recover what can be recovered.

Fighting Sadness

I set down my human-created problems by going outdoors.
I feel my mood immediately lift as I walk in nature.

If I find myself in a black mood, the situation improves almost immediately when I step outside. I remember that the sky still shelters the earth, that the wind still whips around the trees, that the grass still grows beneath my feet. The human-created problems of civilization disappear, and I become an organism in the environment. I think it would be better to walk outside in a downpour of heavy rain than to stay inside and feel sad. We are not meant to be stationary information processors but living, social animals.

Today you may be feeling a bit blue. Perhaps things are not going as you planned. Steal some minutes on your lunch break (which should really be called an "exercise break" or an "outdoors break") to walk around, preferably somewhere without a lot of billboards and distractions. See if you do not return, after walking a mile or a few miles, feeling much better.

Avoiding Avoidance

When I find myself delaying good and necessary activities,
I will investigate my avoidance and procrastination.
I will use mindfulness to get myself back on track.

Fear of the dentist only leads to cavities, bad teeth, and, eventually, no teeth. The one way to avoid the dentist's drill or getting dentures is to go to the dentist regularly. Similarly, I tell my boys that if they don't want to clean their room for hours on Saturday, all they have to do is clean their room a little bit every day during the week. Of course, most full-grown adults don't practice this kind of rational portioning of unpleasant activities, so it's not surprising that kids wouldn't either.

Today you may find yourself employing avoidance strategies. It's okay—we all do it. As you sit in silence, just notice the avoidance behavior and any feelings of an emotional fix that you get from procrastination. For example, you may be amused by a particular website, but it's not exactly in line with your priorities. At the end of the meditation, commit just five minutes to doing what you feel you should be doing.

Leaving Guilt Behind

I recognize guilt as an ineffective coping strategy. I acknowledge guilt as a lack of clarity within myself and a lack of communication with those I love. I work constructively to make my life align with my priorities, without resenting others.

When it comes down to it, guilt doesn't make a very good motivator. I can feel guilty about something, but that just magically substitutes an emotion for an action. If I guilt myself or if someone else makes me feel guilty, this produces resentment over the long term, as my stated preferences conflict with my real preferences. I can diffuse the guilt by either taking the action that I don't feel like taking or by just getting clear about my real priorities. The first step toward healing is to recognize the presence of the guilt and move into a more beneficial mental state.

Perhaps you are having feelings of guilt today. Somewhere you have not fully communicated with yourself or with some loved one. Observe the guilt and the situations in which it typically arises. Resolve to find more constructive ways of dealing with these situations. An inspiration may come to you out of the blue, if not now, then later in the day.

Emotional Intelligence

I place no feelings off limits, and I open myself to the full range of human experience. I allow myself openness and honesty about my feelings.

Good cooking combines all of the different flavors: sweet, sour, salty, bitter, and umami. In the same way, a full emotional life contains traces of happiness and anger, joy and sorrow. We commonly think of happiness as *good* and sadness or anger as *bad*, but no emotion is really bad unless it becomes the default setting. What kind of person wouldn't want to be sad when a friend dies, or angry at some injustice? A healthy emotional life just means having emotions appropriate to the situation.

Take a look at your emotional life here in this safe, quiet space. Do you see a particular feeling or range of feelings dominating your life? Are there feelings that you have placed off limits that you will not allow yourself to feel? Open your heart and mind to the full range of human experience. Give yourself the courage to flow more freely with your emotions. See yourself becoming a little more vulnerable, a little more honest about your feelings.

The Gift of Time

*I make myself aware of the short duration of this lifetime,
and I cultivate gratitude for the time that I have. I use my time to
the best of my ability, expressing love for those around me and serving
the larger community to which I belong.*

We have all been given the gift of time. Of all things, time can be taken for granted the most easily. We usually don't realize the beauty of life until it is under threat in some way, as in the case of illness or injury. It is possible to become mindful of the brevity of life through meditation. We can, through a process of reflection, realize the limited duration of our time on earth. Some great yogis and saints have even been given exact knowledge of the time of their death in advance. Even if we do not have access to this occult knowledge, we can keep finitude in mind and make the best of the time that we have. We can especially make sure to express love and serve the communities to which we belong.

Today, become aware of your own duration within the larger flow of time. Pay attention to the cycles of nature and the temporal flows within your own body. Look at your life cycle and your current place within it. Feel a sense of the vastness of space and time and your own limited part within this expanse. Allow gratitude to emerge within the heart chakra, and let it enfold you.

Setting Things in Motion

I take my good intentions and channel them into positive action in the world. As good thoughts become good actions, the deepest intentions of my heart become reality.

Good intentions alone do not create change. In order for real transformation to happen, we must change the thought processes while taking positive action in the world. We have to create a virtuous cycle where thought, word, and deed all align in the same direction. Thought, word, and deed all fall under the general concept of karma or action. As the Bhagavad Gita states, we must not be attached to action or to inaction. We set things in motion the best way that we know, and then allow the outcomes to fall as they will.

As you sit here in quiet, take note of any contrary states of mind. See the places of willfulness, the places of fear, the places where you resist change. Imagine those places of resistance dissolving. See your mental and physical energies being channeled into the projects most dear to your heart. See every obstacle falling away as you make your heart's desire come to life in the world.

Holy Stubbornness

I dig in my heels for my highest belief. I cling to an unreasonable vision of a more perfect world, and I align my actions with that perfect vision.

We like to make self-control mysterious and difficult, but it really is just a matter of taking a stubborn disposition and turning it to good ends. If we can dig in our heels out of spite or self-will, we can also dig in our heels for compassion and surrender. We can see a vision of the way that we would like the world to be and doggedly pursue that end through all seasons, even when it seems to be going nowhere. We have to set reason aside and go with that tenacity that flies in the face of reason.

Allow your ideal vision of the world to emerge in your mind's eye. See this vision in all clarity and detail. Imagine what it would be like to pursue this vision with determination, day after day, year after year. Commit yourself to this vision, even if it never comes to fruition in your lifetime. Imagine yourself feeling satisfied, knowing that you did all that you could to realize the best that you have within you.

The Mast Year

I know that I will have lean years and bountiful years, years when I am weak and years when I am strong. I give thanks for thick and thin, knowing that every cycle has its purpose.

Every third year or so, oak trees will have what is called a mast year, when the acorn crop will be much more bountiful than usual. This does not simply have to do with the amount of rainfall during the spring but serves an evolutionary purpose. During that year, there will be so many acorns that the squirrels, the deer, and the birds will not be able to eat them all. That will lead to a crop of oak saplings to cover the forest floor. During the lean years (which keep the forager populations down), a few of those saplings will grow toward maturity.

As you look back on your years of meditative practice, you may see some lean years and some years of plenty. You may have some harsh judgments on your mind for the years when you practiced less often. Release these unforgiving sentiments, knowing that everything has natural variability. You will come to complete maturity when the time is right. Just keep reaching toward the light. Year after year, reach toward the light.

The Inner Chamber

I bring my awareness to the expansive inner space.
I allow the divine light to shine throughout my being.

Live from the interest, not from the principal. Create an inner storehouse of energy that you constantly replenish. Do not work heedlessly, but pay close attention to the inner state. Keep mind, heart, and hands synchronized. If your mind begins to get foggy, take a break. Go outside or do some deep breathing. You can only push through the difficulty for so long until it begins to deplete your reserves. Everything will come together in due time.

Sit with your spine as straight as you are physically able. Pay attention to the spinal column and make it more spacious. Feel the strength and surety there. Withdraw the senses into the spine, as though it were a large, cylindrical room, a chamber big enough to hold anything. Then picture a shaft of brilliant light going up this room and into the sky above. Expand the inner space, and feel the outer space recede.

The Great, Unseen Community

I recognize my communion with the great, unseen community of people seeking peace throughout the world. I renounce infatuation with the privileged and powerful and cast my lot with common people.

Right now, people throughout the world, of all faiths and backgrounds, pursue greater peace and understanding in their lives. This one great, unseen community holds the fabric of society together and makes the world more sane and livable. Forget the titans of industry and the political class: everyday people really make the world function. Common decency and hard work are the foundations of society, not financial manipulation and mass entertainment. A single street vendor has more worth to society than all of the billionaires in the world put together.

Today, as you sit in silence, think of all of the people every day who you may be taking for granted. Think of the person who serves you coffee, the person who sweeps the floor. Think of the people who empty your trash and those who work with their hands. Give thanks for these people and make them visible in your mind's eye. Wish them wealth and success, health and happiness. When you open your eyes, take one small action to make life better for ordinary people.

Going Against the Grain

I claim my power to make a better life for myself. I work to build a more compassionate society for all people.

Industrial societies have many built-in pathologies. These consumer societies make unhealthy, processed food cheap and widely available, while keeping healthy, fresh food expensive and hard to obtain. These societies stack people in cubicles and seal them in automobiles, keeping them from getting adequate sunshine and exercise. These societies emphasize productivity and efficiency above the human values of care and concern. To live mindfully means proactively working against the grain of society, to choose a better life and work to build a more just world.

Today, as you breathe deeply and cultivate contentment, feel a firm resolution building in yourself to insist on a more healthy and peaceful way of life. Let go of the old story that you must passively accept whatever society sends your way. Know, from the depths of your being, that you are an agent of transformation. Give yourself permission to craft a beautiful life for yourself and your community.

Invitation to Inclusion

I refuse to allow racism and xenophobia to overtake the values of kindness and compassion. I redirect my life toward the inclusion of the weakest members of society. I allow love to transform my life.

Racism and xenophobia are on the march in Europe and the United States. Such attitudes are antithetical to the practice of mindfulness, as these ideologies perpetuate false boundaries between people and nations. The person who sees clearly rejects nationalism and racism as destructive fictions and is willing to take risks to include and invite oppressed minorities into full participation in society. To fail to practice inclusion is to lack compassion and kindness, the guiding values of the mindfulness movement.

As you sit here in relative quiet at midday, feel a great warmth and love arising in your heart. Surrender to this tremendous power of love, and allow it to amend your thoughts and actions. Allow the inner wellspring to suffuse your life with ease and tranquility.

Positive Masculinity

I envision a new masculinity based on wisdom rather than domination. I support men in the quest to find positive outlets for emotional expression that will allow the transformation of human relations.

Traditional masculinity boasts braggadocious talk and indiscriminate violence above the dignified speech and loving stance of positive masculinity. Men, especially men in positions of privilege, have a lot of learning to do in the coming century. This learning centers on the concept of honor. Men need to learn to honor both their own feelings and the divine feminine in their lives. This has nothing whatever to do with perpetuating patriarchy, but with building diverse communities of loving concern. A sacred masculinity must emerge that is based on wisdom rather than domination.

Take a moment here in the silence to acknowledge the harms that negative visions of masculinity have caused in your life. Look for the hurt in your own heart, perhaps caused by abuse or emotional distance. Do not suppress the emotions but allow them to come out into the light. Honor and respect any feelings that arise, without necessarily magnifying or reinforcing them.

Learning to Love the Body

I accept my body as my vehicle through life. I care for the body in the best way that I know, honoring it on this short journey through my present incarnation.

When I was a kid, we used to make little folded paper boats and float them down the neighborhood stream. They would tumble down rapids, swirl in eddies, and eventually get waterlogged and no longer float. The human body is like that little paper boat. It goes along joyfully through the rapids of life and then, at some point, slowly or all of a sudden, it no longer works. We must learn to love our bodies while we have them, whether they work well or not at the moment.

Perhaps today you are feeling pain in some part of your body or hating some aspect of your physical form. Take the time now to notice the pain or discomfort. Notice the sensations of your body in intimate detail. Send feelings of love and appreciation toward your body, especially the parts that are causing you the most discomfort. Notice the temporary nature of your body, and resolve to take care of it while you can, to the best of your ability.

Midday Pause

I give myself the gift of a pause at midday.
I allow my mind and spirit to be rejuvenated by this silent time.

Taking a break in the middle of the day is not a crime. It will not even make you less productive. You will not miss anything, except for a few trivial web links that you might have clicked. So stop rushing for a few minutes. Give yourself the gift of calm at midday. Your work will not suffer in the least. Your mind will be refreshed, and your spirit will be renewed. There is no merit to grinding your nerves raw: rest and contemplate, if only for a little while.

As you sit in the silence, you may feel a racing feeling, like you have just gotten off a carnival ride. Notice the uncomfortable feeling of sitting still, the urge to do something, anything. Feel that tug to go back to the world. Observe it closely and acquaint yourself with that craving for stimulation. Sit with it until it fades into the background. When that feeling has been truly tamed and defeated, you will be able to work with a mind and heart that are in perfect synchronicity.

Grinding the Wheat of Devotion

I hold a mantra in my hand, and my heart sings.
My beloved one taught me this song, and I sing it even now.
This song began before the world, and it makes my feet dance.

Sai Baba of Shirdi, an Indian saint belonging to both the Muslim and Hindu traditions, once kept cholera out of the village by grinding wheat and sprinkling the flour around the perimeter of the dwellings. We grind the wheat of devotion by reading scriptures and singing devotional songs, by studying philosophy and sitting in silent contemplation. We then spread the fruits of our practices—the patience and joy—to the people and things we love, in order to keep out the cholera of the spirit, the wasting sicknesses of anger and depression.

There is a little bit of work to meditation. We have to work at it every day, just a little more, to get stronger, to increase the patience and concentration. Whatever time that you spent in *sadhana* (spiritual practice) yesterday, see if you can do a little more today. Try also to increase the intensity of the practice, and be a little more strict with yourself. Don't worry about whether or not it is working: just allow things to happen as they may.

What Is Holding Me Back?

I investigate the psychological barriers to my creative and spiritual success.
I overcome these barriers by taking small steps in the here and now.

The most common excuses that we give ourselves for delaying any important undertaking have to do with what we lack: "I don't have enough time" and "I don't have enough money." These all-purpose psychological barriers prevent us from taking the simple steps that can improve our lives. We need to drop the grand plans and ambitions and stick to the ground right under our feet, to begin with ten minutes and ten dollars and move upward from there.

Today, ask yourself what you gain by not taking the steps to transform your life. You may fear giving up some of your less-than-optimal habits in order to stimulate your creative and spiritual growth. Ask yourself, "What is holding me back?" See what arises for you as you ask yourself this question. Then commit to martialing your resources to overcome the obstacle.

Inside Out

I move my mind, and then I move the world.
All things can be overcome by first setting the mind into a good disposition.

When trouble arises in my life, I think of two things: Ganesha and my gurus. The Lord and my teachers have shown me the way to overcome trouble, by working from the inside out. I start with my mental states using mantra and meditation. As I move my mind into a better place, it then becomes much easier to move the world around me. If my mind is not in a good state, I will surely fail to see the opportunities available to me in the physical world. If my mind is in a good state, all manner of adverse conditions can be overcome.

Begin today's meditation by thinking of your chosen divinity. If you consider yourself atheist or agnostic, simply think of the person who most exemplifies the type of life that you would like to lead. Hold your chosen exemplar in your mind's eye as you meditate. You may allow your imagination some free rein. Alternate between silence and reflection upon your chosen ideal. You may receive some words of advice or helpful imagery to guide you through the difficulties that you face.

The Genius Within

Genius comes from the mind, which I use as a tool. I will not seek outside myself what can be found within, or give credit to things where the mind is at work.

When it comes to the use of substances, whether we are talking about alcohol or caffeine or harder drugs, including prescription medications, creative spiritual practitioners may be fooled into thinking that the substance really does the work. But no cup of coffee has ever written a book or a play, and heroin has never made a single person into a musical genius. Substance abuse is the bane of the creative life, not its muse. The human mind is the real miracle, the real source of genius. Remember this and live. Forget this and die an early death.

Take a look now at your own life and any addictions that may be holding you in chains. Imagine for a few minutes what it would be like to go without your favorite addiction for a day or a week or a lifetime. Consider the possibility that what you take to be your muse and inspiration may actually be the source of your trouble. Open your mind to the possibility for change in your life, even a very small and gradual change.

Ajna Chakra Meditation

I concentrate my mind on the point between the brows, and thoughts depart. I let go of the contents of consciousness and rest in bare awareness.

The ajna chakra that rests between the eyes is located just in front of the optic chiasm, where the nerves to the left and right eye cross on their way to the occipital region of the brain, which processes visual input. The chakra is also located between the two hemispheres of the brain, which are linked via the corpus callosum. The meaning is clear: what we call thought or mind occurs via dialogue between interlocutors. The two eyes, the left-right symmetry of the body, the two halves of the brain—thought emerges from dialogue, from pairing, from opposites.

As you meditate today, visualize the letter V on your forehead, stopping between the brows. Fix the inner sight on this point. You may begin to feel a heat or tingling sensation as you focus your mind on this one spot. The laser-like intensity of your gaze will burn any thoughts that may arise. If you feel concentration beginning to wane, you may chant *Aum Vishnu*.

Giving and Action

I will not passively sit back and wait for gifts to drop from heaven. I will consciously and deliberately move in the direction of my dreams.

There is a weak and ineffective form of prayer that asks God for favors and gives nothing in return. This mode of prayer weakens human agency while dishonoring the divine. Life truly begins to change when we pursue the path of action, in which we take concrete steps toward the goals that we want to see realized. This should be accompanied by giving, in the form of ritual worship or charitable activity. In this manner, we both honor divinity and allow our own dreams to come to fruition.

Have you been expecting God to give you things while not lifting a finger yourself? Take a few minutes to sit in the divine majesty of this moment, cultivating a sense of gratitude. Ask yourself what it would look like if you put yourself wholeheartedly into realizing your dreams. Ask yourself what you are willing to give in order to express your gratitude to God (or your own personal version of the mystery of life).

Enlighten Up

I reject martyrdom as a way of life.
I believe that my spiritual practice makes my life more joyful and complete.

One of the side effects of spiritual practice is taking oneself too seriously, as though wearing a dour face could lead to enlightenment. Spirituality—if the word means anything—should help us to learn to play and laugh, to live creatively and freely. If spirituality leads to emotional turbulence, to harsh and judgmental attitudes, to denigration of the life of the flesh, it isn't worthwhile or good. Spirituality should help us to live life more fully, to love being alive. If it doesn't do that, we should let it go.

Do you equate spirituality with seriousness, with harsh discipline, with self-harm? Take a few minutes to imagine a spirituality of merriment, of fun, of joy. Allow joy to suffuse your being. Allow the load to be lifted from your heart. Feel your cares and concerns becoming lighter. See yourself overcoming all adverse circumstances and getting in touch with your deepest purpose.

Poverty and Plenty

I realize that poverty and plenty complete each other, that each is a modification of the other. This realization frees me from craving, and I rest in whatever condition I find myself.

During my time in college and graduate school, I ate a lot of ramen noodles. They cost a dollar for six packages, and, when paired with a can of Veg-All, they made for a full stomach on the cheap. At the time, I thought this was rather ingenious, as though I had found a loophole in the grocery store price structure. Looking back on it, I was probably malnourished and certainly had consumed far too much sodium and preservatives. I am grateful now to be able to afford fresh food and a roof over my head. And yet those times also made me what I am today.

Today you may find yourself struggling, or you may be in the midst of plenty. Realize that these opposites complete each other and bleed into one another. Follow this chain of reflection to know the instability of all oppositions: while plenty and poverty are not the same, they do partake of the same structure. Knowing one, you also know its opposite. As you sit here in this place, hold all opposition in suspension, and know that all of the potentialities are available for you, here and now.

Two Attitudes about Money

I will not fall into either loving money or loathing it.
I will complete my work diligently, but not obsessively,
knowing that the resources I need are coming my way.

There are two attitudes about money and possessions that are unhelpful. The first attitude makes money into a number-one priority in life and a primary measure of success. If this attitude is held long enough, it will become self-destructive, as health, relationships, and fun are put on hold indefinitely to chase the almighty dollar. An equally unhelpful attitude is being lackadaisical or scornful of money, as though it were not necessary to be concerned about it at all. This equally will lead to suffering eventually, because money can give us food, shelter, and medicine that we need. Most of us vacillate between these poles, but we should try to be somewhere in the middle.

You may find that you have an overly passionate relationship with money in one direction or the other. Breathe into these passionate thoughts and feelings as you sit in meditation. Allow calm to come into your mind and heart. See yourself working confidently, able to satisfy all of your needs with a modicum of effort.

The Perfect Day

I choose to take care of myself, and that doesn't make me a bad person. As I take care of my own needs, I feel more generous and giving with others.

Today you may be facing deadlines given to you by other people, like your colleagues or your boss. You may have work to do that doesn't feel very satisfying or interesting. Before you get to these pressing but tedious duties, take a few minutes to do what you want to do. Go for a walk or draw a picture or read a book. When you have taken care of yourself for a little bit, you will feel much less resentful of the work that needs to be done. Then logically break down the task into small steps and take care of it.

You may be putting other people first in your life, only to feel constantly resentful and strained. As you sit here in meditation, imagine what the perfect day would look like from your perspective. Sit here for a few minutes basking in the feeling of that perfect day. When you open your eyes, take a few concrete steps to bring your life into greater alignment with your vision.

Thousands and Thousands

I look into the tangled knots of my own life,
and I do not see an unsolvable problem. I see a mystery
waiting to be unlocked. I untangle the threads not only for myself,
but for those who came before me and those who will come after me.

A thousand feet have marched before you, and a thousand will march after you have gone. This worn pathway that you now tread has its ghosts, and its angels as well. If you learn to solve this mystery of your own life, you will help countless others to find their way as well. Become an inspiration for yourself, and you will also be an inspiration for others. You may not know where you are going or what you are doing, but if you look deep within, past all doubt and confusion, you will find the way to the place where you are going.

As you turn inward this day, you may feel weary of the world. Look deep into the heart to find that spark of love and truth and beauty. As you *in-spire* with the breath, feel the new ideas coming into your mind. Feel a new peace and compassion coming into your heart. See yourself becoming the person you were always meant to be. Do not doubt that the life of your dreams is within your reach. You have not made any mistakes: everything has been for the greater purpose of your realization.

Walking in the Dark

I need not have all of the solutions at my disposal.
I only need the dim outlines of a course of action.

If you find yourself bumbling around in the dark, it is best to let your eyes adjust before proceeding. The dim outlines of things appear where previously there had been only blackness. In the dark times in our lives, it can be easy to be reactive, like a person stumbling. Mindfulness helps us to adjust, to see clearly in dark times. Then we can plan a more constructive response that takes full stock of the situation at hand.

Maybe things look bleak now, but take a few minutes to sit here in the figurative darkness. Let your thoughts and emotions settle. Separate *what is* from *what is not*. You don't need to have a fully formed plan of life: you only need the dim outlines. Look now: possibilities emerge where there were none. Carefully go back to your own life. See in the dark.

Easy and Light

I will find a place of ease and comfort in my work. I will find that weightless place where I lose track of time and things get done almost by magic.

The good work that you were really born to do will not feel difficult. It will come quite easily, as easily as breathing. The time will pass quickly when you have found the work of your lifetime. People around you will be kvetching and complaining, but you will feel serene. You will sometimes feel like it is almost criminal that you could make a living doing what you really love. If you don't have this feeling of ease, of lightness in your work, at least some of the time, you may need an adjustment in your work.

Think back to the last time you felt really at ease in your work, like you were doing something fun and easy, but also deeply meaningful. Now ask yourself how you could have that feeling today. Forget for a little bit about money and practicality. At the end of your time of meditation, go and do that easy and light thing that makes you happy.

Small Changes

I make small adjustments in the direction of my dreams.
I take many small risks that lead to big changes over time.

The smallest changes in your routine can have ripple effects that change your entire world. You sit next to a new person at lunch. You take a little more care with your wardrobe. You learn a new technical skill. Suddenly a small change leads to another small change, and, eventually, you find yourself in a completely different place. The linear curve, without warning, becomes an exponential curve. The workaday self becomes a rock star all of a sudden.

You may have doubts about your capacity to change your life. You need not defeat these doubts entirely; just don't let them have the final say, the veto power. See the doubt clearly in your mind, and then disobey it. Perhaps you can name some doubts right now, so that you can recognize them the next time they arise.

In Good Company

I sit here keeping company with myself, building the inner treasure.
I undertake the work of faithfulness to my deepest vision,
even when no one comes with me.

No one else will come to your rescue to help you live the life of your dreams. Even people who genuinely love you will likely not understand your priorities, and, even if they do understand, will be powerless to help. Transformation happens only through daily effort, and, at least at first, through solitary effort. Eventually you find working partners, allies who can help your plans come to fruition. In the meantime, it's just you and the yoga mat, you and the sketchbook, you and the keyboard, you and the gym.

Meditation teaches you to be alone without being uncomfortable. As you sit here keeping company with yourself, realize just how much is happening beneath the surface. Your mind contains a symphony. You have a plethora of skills and abilities. So being here alone need not be fearful or boring. Just sit here in good company.

Balancing Career and Spirituality

I do not have to choose between my spirituality and my work.
I choose to integrate my belief system into my work,
so that I might become a whole person.

Many wealthy and powerful people have no inner happiness and leave behind a string of failed relationships. Conversely, many people who might not be considered successful are emotionally stable and have good family lives. This is not to say that wealth is inherently corrupting, only that the inner and outer work are two separate tasks. Creative spiritual practitioners cultivate tranquility within, but they also fully understand the need for ordinary work in the world. A well-balanced person will practice meditation but will also do the things necessary (within the bounds of ethics) to succeed in life, keeping always in mind that success is relative and context dependent.

As you look at your life, you may find yourself veering wildly between self-care and opportunism. After five to ten minutes of silent contemplation, imagine what it would look like for your spiritual self and your material wishes to completely coincide. Ask Lord Ganesha or your chosen divinity to make this vision a reality.

Meditation and Sensuality

I give thanks for life in the flesh; I enjoy the pleasures of this incarnation.
I keep always mindful of the good things in life that bring delight.

Dharmic philosophy does not look down on sexuality or the pleasures of food and drink. Pleasure in itself does not present a problem; in fact, it is one of the aims of life. Pleasure only becomes a problem when it prevents one from seeking enlightenment or when it comes in the way of acting justly. Otherwise, it is perfectly acceptable, outside of monastic life, to indulge in enjoyment of the senses. Mindfulness actually enhances sensual enjoyment by getting rid of the mental obstructions to living in the present.

You may have in your past a tendency to feel guilty about your carnal existence. Become more aware of your body right now. Picture the storehouses of wisdom opening to you, as though this earthly frame held hidden repositories of knowledge. Open your mind to the possibility that your body might become your teacher.

Small Luxuries

I give myself the things I need to support my practice. I expend energy in order to invite the divine into my life.

Giving your spiritual practice some nurturing can help you move to the next level. Invest in incense of higher quality, a better meditation cushion, some traditional clothing, an image of your deity or guru, a set of ritual items. Offer flowers, fruit, fire, and water. Welcome God as a guest in your home by creating the atmosphere of reverence. Take care of your home to the best of your ability. Take care of your body to the best of your ability. These things help to invite divinity into your life.

If you are feeling depressed today, lacking energy, take a look at your relationship to physical space. If you need to, take a few minutes to declutter, and then come back to the meditation space. You may find that you are better able to concentrate if you have a basic level of order around you.

The Third Space

I open myself to the spine-tingling protrusion of divinity into my life.
I seek the disruption that only the things of the spirit can bring.

You will have little glimpses of eternity strewn along your path as you pursue the path of inner cultivation. You will notice beauty in your everyday life that would have previously escaped notice. Let these little signs become encouragement to delve deeper, to risk a little more, and to take the practice further. Allow your practice of meditation to go from being a mild form of stress relief to becoming a major part of your life. Look upon the practice as being just as important as your career or your marriage, a sort of third space between work and home.

Congratulations on having taken this time in the middle of your day to center yourself in this sacred space. Allow yourself the attitude, the spiritual feeling, of total victory. Know that the same power of will that has taken you thus far will take you all the way to complete freedom. Know in your heart of hearts that you are destined for complete and everlasting bliss.

Pure Light Being

I shift my energy from the conquering attitude to the self-poised attitude.
All good things come to me as I sit in illuminated awareness.

Some self-help books share an aggressive outlook: that one must have an iron-clad will and work with great intensity to impose one's vision upon the world. In the yogic philosophy, this quality of self-assertion is known as rajas, the passionate nature. While this tendency must be present in nature, it is considered the intermediate energy. The higher energy is called sattva, which denotes clarity, tranquility, and light. Sattva is believed to propel evolution in a more efficient manner, as it eliminates the desiring aspect.

As you examine your mind and heart at midday, you may have a lingering belief that you must exhaust yourself financially, emotionally, or physically in order to achieve your life goals. Look into the core of your being and see the areas where you may be depleted; fill these ragged, torn areas with the pure light of expansive consciousness.

Feeling versus Reality

I recognize that my feelings may not be a reliable guide to my progress in life. I concentrate on the work at hand rather than wishing for a better future.

You may be frustrated today that you don't feel any special sense of bliss or don't feel any sense of accomplishment. Keep in mind that you can't necessarily see all of the fruits of your actions. You don't have access to the full picture within normal conscious awareness. You shoot the arrows of karma but don't see them land. Keep the attention on doing what you can rather than trying to predict the outcome. Work deftly but blindly, trusting that every deed will reap results.

As you enter this space of meditation, you may see the phantoms of self-pity, discouragement, and doubt. Mentally turn away from the false consolations of these emotional states. See them dissolve like the mist before the light of awareness. You need only notice them, and they will go away. These false friends stand in the way of your awakening.

Hare Mind, Tortoise Mind

I carry my home with me wherever I go.
I stay with this moment and do not rush ahead.

Aesop's fable of the tortoise and the hare can be just as profound as any wisdom literature. The point is not just that the turtle goes slowly but that the turtle goes steadily and deliberately in his activity, while the hare goes quickly and exhausts himself. Creative people in any field can learn from this ancient parable: a little bit of work done every day will be better than random, frenzied spurts. The same holds true in meditation and spirituality: the practitioner, like the turtle, makes progress by slow gains.

You may have a turtle mind today or a hare mind. In order to slow down the mind, pay attention to the pull of gravity on your body, settling your spinal column into the sit bones. You don't need to stop the flow of thoughts: just picture this flow getting heavier and more viscous. When you emerge from your shell at the end of meditation, plod steadily throughout your day.

The Power of Choice

My choices have great power over the direction of my life.
I steer thought, word, and deed toward my chosen goal.

We do not have a choice about whether or not to think, or whether or not to act. Just by being alive, we are bound to some sort of action. We only have a choice about the nature of that action and what we choose to be the ideal pattern for our lives. We will live the life of our choosing, so we must be careful about that choice.

You may notice some defeatist notions today. If those notions were put to words, they might be: "Nothing I do makes a difference," or "My life will never amount to anything." This frustration will not last unless you will it to last. Take away its support and it will fall apart of its own accord. As you take this midday break, check to see if you are living according to your best intentions. You have been given the opportunity to make a course correction whenever you want.

Beyond Procrastination

I wrestle with the most slippery and devious beast of all, my own mind.
I catch this beast in its own traps, and I achieve victory.

Procrastination comes in many forms. It can take the form of endlessly exploring the different options, working on something trivial rather than something important, getting lost in entertainment, making plans for action rather than actually acting, and many other variations along these lines. No sooner have you defeated one form of procrastination than another form takes its place. The only way out of procrastination is to go ahead and do the really hard but important thing, if only for a few minutes.

As you sit here in the space of meditation, you may feel a twinge of guilt at something left undone. If the task is laden with anxiety, break it down in your mind into as many parts as possible. Then think of the very first step, which could be very easy. As soon as you leave your meditation, go and take that first step.

Sweet and Bitter

I accept the pairs of opposites as part of one and the same reality. I release the need for complete control over my life and accept things as they come.

Life may be bitter and disappointing today. This downside, this depressing part of life, cannot be eliminated. The bitterness is part and parcel of the sweetness in life: the two go together. What appear to us as opposites depend on each other and are defined by each other. The world will always have both good and evil, honest people and crooked people. The mysterious truth is that both are necessary, and beyond their apparent opposition is a higher good that transcends our understanding.

Your mind may be fighting now against some personal affront, against some minor disaster. Work on releasing the tight grip of the mind on the bitter problem at hand. Smooth the lines in your furrowed brow and let the tight jaw loosen. Let go of the negative emotions, as though you were freeing a caged bird. Open the chest, open the heart chakra, and allow the kundalini energy to rise through the crown of the head. Keep working at it until you know the sweetness of peace.

Tired but Not Defeated

When difficult times come, I turn my thoughts away from things of this world. I look within for the hidden treasure.

Today you may be feeling bone-tired, like you have been working for countless years, only to see your efforts come to nothing. You struggle with debt, with poor health, with family troubles, and nothing ever seems to improve. At times like this, you can best practice detachment, as you see clearly that the world is full of troubles. As you release your grip on worldly bonds, you see the divine more clearly. The bliss of pure being opens to you as soon as you begin to look for it.

Today, sit in silent expectation for at least twenty to thirty minutes. Try to concentrate on complete receptivity, on listening as intently as possible. Let your whole mind and body be attuned to this place and time. You may have some sort of epiphany or you may not, but stay with the experience. Resist the temptation to yield to an inner monologue or to label and define the experience. Avoid reflecting on the past or fantasizing about the future.

Good Health

*I give myself the luxury of good health. Caring for my mind
and body pays big dividends, both now and in the future.*

We try to make healthy living into some big mystery so that we don't have to take responsibility for our habits. Health advice varies greatly in the particulars, but the big constants remain the same: avoid eating too much sugar and processed food, eat lots of fruits and vegetables, and get plenty of exercise. We have a tendency to think of exercise as optional, but it is necessary for a healthy mind and body. A person who does not exercise will be unhealthy, physically and emotionally.

To quickly gain better health, beginning today, think of your lunch break as an exercise break that also involves some food. Go to the gym if you can; if you can't, go for a long walk. Take two-thirds of your break for exercise and one-third for food. Do both your exercise and your eating mindfully: pay attention to the way your body feels as you treat it well.

Personal Health Goals

I do not force myself to conform to an idealized body image. I form a picture of health that is unique to me alone, and I make that my goal.

We tend to get our ideas about health from published articles and pictures. Some of these ideas can be useful, but they also portray idealized versions of reality. The airbrushed pictures of models with perfect bodies lead to despondency instead of inspiration. We have to move from asking what is healthy in general to asking what is healthy for me at this point in my life. From this personalized picture of health, we can begin to move into better habits.

If you don't have any health goals, think about the time in your life when you felt the best, emotionally and physically. Think about what you would have to do to get back to that same level of health, and plan accordingly. Immediately excuses will arise. Sort through them, one by one, to determine if they are legitimate concerns. If you have any chronic conditions, you may have to make some adaptations. But don't let your health problems become an excuse for not exercising at all, as this only leads to further deterioration.

Care versus Deprivation

I give my body the things that it needs to be well. I do not treat it harshly, but gently guide it into better patterns.

When most people begin to lead a healthier lifestyle, often the first thing they do is stop eating all the foods that they really like. The mind, of course, immediately rebels and starts conjuring thoughts of the forbidden foods. The diet may last days or even weeks, but eventually the old ways come back again. Only through a whole-life approach, involving meditation and mindfulness, ayurveda (holistic alternative medicine) and Western medicine, and varied forms of exercise, can the change become permanent.

The mind of a fully grown human being is, in certain ways, not unlike the mind of a child. It is loss averse and does not want to have its candy taken away. Today, speak nicely to the mind and body, saying, "Don't worry, I will take care of you. I will not do anything that is going to harm you. I will make these changes gradually, and you will have plenty of time to adjust. And I promise you that you will feel much better when I'm done!"

Food and Emotions

I look for positive outlets for my emotions. As I express myself constructively, I have less need to self-medicate through food.

Many poor food choices really have nothing to do with food. They have to do with being bored and frustrated in life. The food is a little fix, a small thrill that could just as easily be had by shoplifting, gambling, or drinking. This energy must be redirected toward something truly constructive and creative, like writing, painting, or drawing. Creative outlets are extremely good in tapping into those suppressed emotions. Actually do something with them rather than self-medicating with food or other substances.

Try some new creative outlet today. Pick up some paints or colored pencils or play a musical instrument. Do this totally in secret: no one has to see your work. Let this be your own time, and keep it to yourself, at least for now. Any new pursuit needs some time to mature before it can be shown to others. You may feel strong emotions emerging: allow them to be channeled into the work rather than suppressing them.

Working with Pain

I pay attention to my pain, learning to read its messages. I recognize that some types of pain can be beneficial for my healing.

When you have pain resulting from some injury, the sensible thing to do is to avoid doing anything to aggravate the pain. This good short-term strategy becomes harmful in the long run, as it leads to a later loss of function. Catering to the pain only leads to more pain. It is just as bad to have too little movement as it is to have too much. Your doctor will likely say that some exercise of the affected area will be necessary to get back to normal, and this will also entail some pain. We must learn how to listen to our bodies to gauge the appropriate amount of pain and the right kind of pain.

As you pay attention to your body in this quiet time, you may feel some troublesome spots sending signals of pain. Breathe into the pain and lengthen your body through the problem areas. Picture yourself using the injured limb or problem area. After you have completed your meditation, give the troubled part of your body a moderate amount of exercise.

Normalizing Pain

I recognize that pain is a normal part of life. I will not flee from it or medicate it away. I let pain become my companion and teacher.

In our consumer societies, we have been conditioned to reach for a bottle of pills at the slightest sign of pain. Usually this begins with over-the-counter medications, but it may eventually lead to prescription medications and even street drugs. We have to take a look at the first link in this chain, the idea that pain is somehow bad and is always to be avoided. We have to stop thinking that the world must revolve around our feelings and recognize that pain is just a normal part of life.

If you are having some pain today, physical or emotional, begin with paying close attention to its signals. It may be that the pain holds a hidden message: that you are working too hard or going too quickly. It may be that your body needs some exercise or nourishment that it is not getting. Rather than trying to make the pain go away, try to learn what it is trying to teach you. Then it will depart quite easily.

Don't Force It

*When something doesn't work in my life, I avoid using aggression
to force things into place. I stop and look for clarity.
I work with gentleness and care to reach a solution.*

We have a part of ourselves that gets impatient, that wants results now. When things don't go our way at work, in relationships, or in some manual task, we may try to force things into place. We use harsh words instead of diplomatic skills, brute force instead of care. When we force things, sometimes they get broken. It would be much better to fully understand the problem before proceeding, to go forward cautiously.

Today you may find yourself in the midst of a situation that doesn't seem to be working. Take a pause now in the midst of your day. Offer up this meditation as a solution to the problem. Picture the problem clearly in your mind's eye, and then go into your place of silent reflection. When you return to your work, a solution will begin to form.

The Signal and the Noise

In the space of inner awareness, I inquire as to what I find to be truly important.
I revise my beliefs in accordance with the deepest yearning of my heart.

As a society, we have become very good at accessing information, but we have regressed in our ability to discern the purpose behind what we do, to find the difference between the signal and the noise. Mindfulness meditation does not tell anyone what to do or what to believe: it gives people the space they need to decide for themselves, apart from the deluge of words and images. In the still, small space of the heart, it becomes easier to spot what we really believe versus what we think we ought to believe.

Think for a moment about the one thing that is most important in the world to you. Now offer that one most important thing up to the light of silent observation. See if it withstands the scrutiny of the inner silence. You may surprise yourself by finding that what you thought was most important is actually in second or third place. Or maybe you just want to revise your priorities slightly. See if you can do this wordlessly, through feelings alone, or perhaps by incorporating a few images.

Learning to Tell the Truth

In the light of awareness, I strive to see things clearly. I do not shrink from the knowledge that is my birthright as an awakened soul.

Have you ever been able to catch someone in a lie? You may not be certain of the exact nature of the lie, but you know that something isn't quite right. The story doesn't quite make sense. Being able to tell when someone is lying is very difficult, even for police detectives. It is even more difficult, but more important, to spot the lies that we tell ourselves. Attaining this inner truthfulness becomes the foundation for everything else we do in life. Once we stop lying to ourselves, it becomes easier to tell the truth to others.

You may have in mind certain beliefs about yourself—your abilities, traits, and dispositions—that may just be convenient fictions. You may err on the side of self-criticism or on the side of boastfulness: both are distortions. Use the interior silence to unflinchingly analyze yourself, seeing things as they are rather than the way you would have them to be. Realize that everything you take for granted is mutable and fleeting. You are not your self-image.

Becoming Simultaneous

I move my awareness fully into this place and time, holding nothing back.

We take too little time to enjoy life and don't even really understand what enjoyment means. In the first place, we are far too concerned about productivity and making money—false, invented measures mistaken for being normal and natural. On top of that, we mistake enjoyment for self-indulgence, having to do with food, sex, drugs, and the like. Enjoyment has an aesthetic dimension, but it need not be hedonistic: it is just about paying attention to the good things in life and savoring them. By that I mean life as is, not some other life out there that we have to chase down. The imagined, ideal life never arrives.

Take this moment, as it has been given to you, and drink deeply from it. Appreciate with all of your faculties—your senses, your feelings, your intellect—this time and place as it appears to you before consciousness. Invest every fiber of your being into staying with this moment. Hold nothing back. See if you can, for even an instant, touch time as it is touching you. Become simultaneous with yourself.

The Long Now

I refuse to die of overcautiousness. I refuse to live halfway. I will build something beautiful of this, my one long and beautiful now.

Today, think: this is it. This is the only today that I have. I have to make the best of it, to wring all of the joy and tears, all of the laughter and adventure and pathos and pain and beauty out of it. I have to make this one count. That means I pull out the stops, let go of the self-imposed limitations, and swing for the fences. I live as myself, however strange that might be. I worship my own gods, recite my own creed, and dance to my own song.

In the light of consciousness, you can almost see the mental limitations that obscure the way forward. When you become very still today, you may sense a feeling of defeatism, of isolation, of smallness. This sense of disconnection must be released: as you let go of these limitations, you will see your connection to everything, each flower, animal, star, and galaxy. You are this. You are the All.

The Subtle Current of Love

I call this place my own. I make the ordinary twists and turns of life my refuge. I find the subtle current of love in the midst of the everyday.

Life cannot really be controlled and managed: like a river, life has contours of its own choosing, rocks just beneath the surface. It eddies and meanders. All of the to-do lists and vision boards in the world cannot tame life. We cannot force the world to conform to our desires. That said, we do have some control over what happens to us. We need the push and the pull, the give and take, the compromise with reality that is human existence. Sometimes we will make a mess, and sometimes we will make something beautiful: usually the reality will fall somewhere between the two.

You may find yourself exhausted by trying to make everything perfect. Rest here in this imperfect space, in this life that is less than you desire. Craft for yourself a little nest made of concentration. Take refuge in this warm space of the heart. Learn to become your own soothing voice, your own mother bird.

Work As an Expression of Love

I turn my work into an expression of love and attention. I pour my whole self into my labor, transforming myself and my world.

I once saw a beetle delving deep in the petals of a magnolia blossom. Its entire body was coated in yellow pollen, but it went on diligently about its work. It was as though the beetle had become part of the flower, as though its whole purpose lay right there in its work among the stamens. I thought about my guru, who spends his entire life chanting ancient Sanskrit hymns, and how the vibrations from these hymns fill his life. He is covered in the pollen from the flowers of the Vedas: he has found his true work. May we all be so lucky!

If you are ever feeling listless and bored, take refuge in your life's work. As you go about your day, try to fill each task with the most love and attention that you can muster. See if you can tell the difference between working robotically and working mindfully. Invest your work with a sense of purpose, even if it's a task that you don't find particularly enjoyable.

Letting Go of Enmity

I will not be defined by the enemies I select for myself.
I surrender all enmity and reclaim my own life.

On the old Warner Bros. cartoon, Wile E. Coyote was always chasing Road Runner with complex stratagems and supplies from the Acme Corporation. No matter what he did, it was always the coyote who ended up jumping off a cliff with an anvil tied to his leg, always the coyote who ended up getting shot with the cannon that he, himself purchased. And yet, the coyote-roadrunner ("Beep! Beep!") dynamic made the show work. When we have enemies in our lives, we may end up going off a cliff: we are just as defined by our enemies as we are by our friends.

Do you have enemies who define you, who chart your course, no matter how much you might wish things to be otherwise? Today, loosen the grip that the other person has on you. Think of how you can let go of those complex stratagems for beating the other person. Think of what it might mean to reclaim your own life, to let go of enmity.

Innate Worth

I am a creature of immense power, beauty, and worth.
I allow my actions to flow from the spotless center of my being.
I do nothing to diminish the inner light that brightens my days.

Do not stop today where you stopped yesterday. Always seek to push just a little farther than you have before. Make your work a little more excellent. Pay more attention in your meditations. Be more kind and caring with your family and friends. Make the world better for the people around you. If you can successfully push beyond the old boundaries on a regular basis, your life will change dramatically in a short period of time. This may sound exhausting at first, but it is only in giving that we gain the energy for renewed growth.

As you sit here in the silence, feel your integrity like a badge of honor on your chest. See this glowing chest plate of polished metal, spotless and new. Feel the divine fullness rising in your chest. Cultivate a feeling of holiness, of spotlessness. Stay with this feeling for a few minutes. Resolve to do nothing today that would subtract from your innate worth.

Great Intelligence
and Simple Love

I share my destiny with the fate of the earth and all living things, and I acknowledge my debts to this earth. I work to fight the politics of exclusion that would rend asunder the bonds between people and nature.

The news often shows a fractured world, full of suffering and pain. But the whole earth and all the creatures living on it comprise one giant organism, with many autoimmune mechanisms, many methods for self-repair. We can bring healing to this one body to which we all belong. We can knit together the broken bonds, repair the damage done to people, animals, and planet by the ravages of individualistic thinking.

Neither extreme optimism nor extreme pessimism is needed. What is needed is great intelligence and simple love: one of these without the other leads to a dead end. Cultivate now great intelligence and simple love, binding together mind and heart. Notice any tendency that would force you to choose between compassion and intellect. Insist on a full synthesis of caring and knowing. Allow your thinking life and your feeling life to become one.

Leaving a Legacy

I leave the world better than it was when I found it. I think of the generations yet to be born, and I direct my life for their benefit.

At the Cathedral of Saint John the Divine in Manhattan, I once had the privilege of seeing stone carvers at work on this magnificent structure. The figures of saints were taking shape from raw slabs of stone. Many of the artisans, I was told, were volunteering their time, just to be able to contribute something to this vast undertaking. It is so rare, these days, to see people thinking in decades or centuries. Everything seems to be about finding the next big score: the future means next week, not the next generation.

Everyone leaves behind a legacy of one kind or another. What will yours be? Bring into your heart center love, generosity, and goodwill. Picture yourself getting bolder in your pursuit of the common good. Expand your consciousness to include generations not yet born, and think of what you would want for them.

Acknowledging Neediness

Gazing inward, I become deeply acquainted with all of my faults and flaws. Bringing these faults into the light of consciousness, I find freedom from them.

Get to know your own neediness, your own wants and desires. If you know what makes you tick, you will be more aware of your vulnerabilities and blind spots. Having this self-awareness is important, not just so that you can craft even better defenses, but so that you can understand what makes your emotional states arise. It then becomes possible to get out of the blame game and accept yourself and other people. Only by knowing ourselves can we stop trying to manipulate others into acting the way that we want them to act.

What is it that you desperately want people to believe about you? See whether this may be the very thing holding you back. Imagine what it would be like if you didn't have to be X, whether that is smart, successful, rich, funny, fashionable, or whatever it is for you. Relieve yourself of that burden, at least for the space of a few minutes. Take that feeling of release with you at the close of your meditation.

Steady Effort

I fix my gaze on the Self now arising.
I labor each day with the vision of the infinite.

The things that you do every day will have far more power than those that you do only occasionally or sporadically. Tasks undertaken daily become automatic, so easy that they require little conscious planning. To accomplish great things, spend some time each day working on the chosen goal. It really is just that simple. A little bit of discipline and constancy will be far more beneficial than the attitude of martyrdom that romantically sacrifices all for the sake of the work. The little bit done daily is far more sustainable than swooning fits of genius.

As you look at your life, you may find yourself burning the candle at both ends. Observe the signs of physical fatigue in your body. Observe the mental fog hanging over you. Imagine yourself doing everything you have ever wanted to do in life, but without feeling tired, without overtaxing yourself. Imagine having physical health, emotional well-being, and yet also living the life of your dreams.

Becoming Radiant

I set aside the bad habit of castigating myself
for perceived faults, and I acknowledge my contributions to the world.
I find my inner radiance and illuminate my world.

Do not make light of your everyday contributions. By lending a listening ear or a helping hand, you can make someone's day or save someone's life. The vast majority of people in the world are just looking for a little bit of understanding and encouragement. When you make yourself strong and steady through spiritual practice, you uphold the world. You become someone's rock of stability, a source of strength and inspiration. Grow into your biggest and strongest self, and save the world. Think the biggest thoughts and take the biggest actions that you can muster.

Our world is composed of millions of fragile bonds between people, things, and nature. As you meditate today, become aware of those myriad bonds that knit you securely into the world. Rather than aggressively seeking to free yourself from these connections, transcend them through love and light. Make yourself so radiant that you illuminate your world.

From Need to Love

I give myself permission to do what I love, to stop seeking a stamp of approval. I find the inner motivation to pursue my work.

We spend most of our lives looking for some sort of validation that never comes, whether that be from our parents, our peers, or some other person in a position of power. Eventually we know that the validation will never arrive, that the magical stamp of having arrived doesn't actually exist. It would be so much better to just do what we love just because we love doing it. The journey from need to love takes quite a long time, and a lot of learning. Eventually we can just be our own weird, wonderful selves without having to worry about it.

As you look within yourself, see what validation you secretly (or not so secretly) crave. Imagine yourself just doing your thing, without the need to prove yourself, without the need to demonstrate your worthiness. See how that changes your work ever so slightly, to be a little more free and loose, to take risks and improvise.

Space for Creativity

I give myself the gift of a space where I can pursue my ideas without criticism. I allow myself to play, to express myself, to create.

Don't let anyone hate on your creative activities, least of all yourself. A poem, a play, a song, a novel, a story, a painting needs room to grow, apart from prying, critical eyes. Allow yourself a garden, some sewing, or knitting. Try a new recipe. Make something with your hands. You can carry on your creative tasks quietly, without making a big stir. The time will come when you are ready to share with others, but you don't have to rush things.

Do you have a workspace, real or virtual, where you can test your crazy ideas? If not, get started on one this very second. If you do have such a space, let your imagination run wild for a little while in the middle of your day. Go ahead and break out the keyboard, the pencils, the paints, the instrument, the microphone. Just be wary of prying eyes.

With or Without Inspiration

When the dry spells come, I keep going despite myself. I walk the trackless wilderness of thought, taking heart that something beautiful awaits me.

Inspiration may help to get things going, but even more important is to continue even when you don't feel inspired. Whether working on a creative project, getting physical exercise, or pursuing meditation, keep going even during the dry spells. Getting into that habit of working a little bit at a time will propel you forward much faster than if you only work when you feel like it.

As you close your eyes and sit here in meditation, you may feel nothing at all. Or you may feel something worse, like depression or despair. Whatever comes, sit there with the thoughts and feelings that arise. Defeat all negative states by staring them down. Shoot the arrows of awareness at the demons of listlessness.

Those Who Have Gone Before

I hold close those who have inspired me in the past, and I do not let their memories die. I hold close their counsel, and my life is enriched.

I think about my grandparents in difficult times. They are all dead now, but I keep their memories alive. I talk to them in the kitchen or on the front porch, in the places that they frequented. I picture my grandfather's blue coveralls, his tins of Prince Albert tobacco. I picture my grandmother with her silver hair, her large Bible. They appear in my dreams from time to time, to give me advice. No one ever told me that I should seek their help or how this should be done: it is just something that came naturally.

Because everything in the universe is interrelated, the effects of everything that has ever been continue to this day. As you close your eyes in this sacred space, you may consult those who have gone before. You don't have to visit a cemetery or hold a séance. All you need to do is imagine them vividly and then start asking questions. Just remember that they are real people, and don't be disrespectful.

The Rope of Time

I open myself to the wisdom that comes to me in the stillness.
I receive the guidance that I need to live life to the fullest.

Picture time like a rope composed of many strands. These strands do not all have the same weight, and they do not all move in the same direction. Some move forward, while others move backward, although these terms are a matter of perspective. It is possible to see into the future, if one can fasten onto one of these subtle strands moving backward (that is, from the future to the past, the arrow of time moving in reverse from our usual perspective). This requires an utterly receptive mind and a strong desire to know. One can get glimpses in this manner, although I think this should be reserved for really important matters.

Think of a question involving the future to which you really need to know the answer. It must be something that really concerns you, something that impinges on your life directly. After spending some time in quiet contemplation, ask your question into the stillness. You may receive an image, a phrase, or even some song lyrics, like a little riddle. See if you do not find an answer to your question.

Now Is the Opportune Time

I press forward with my practice in good circumstances and bad, when it is convenient and when it is inconvenient. I allow mindfulness to disrupt my life.

Do not wait until you feel like meditating. What would happen if you waited until you felt like taking out the trash or felt like paying the bills? The person who makes meditation a regular habit will have more peace of mind all the time, which then frees mental space for other interests, creating a virtuous cycle of increased concentration and enhanced creativity. By contrast, days without meditation lead to a mental fog and emotional frailty, making it difficult to prioritize tasks. With each passing day, the negative states increase.

Before you rush back to your work, take a minute now to center yourself. Feel the sit bones rooted into your seat, your spine balanced and straight atop the muladhara chakra. Inhale deeply and expand the abdomen, the side ribs, and the chest. As the breath expands, move your awareness to the throat and then to the head. Feel a pure light cleansing your thoughts and emotions.

No Shortcuts

I take this time to clear my mind in the middle of the day. I emerge from meditation feeling refreshed, able to work with renewed strength.

I had a brief stint as a prep cook in a fancy restaurant during graduate school. I had to peel and chop potatoes before the dinner rush, and, when dinner started, I would prepare and plate salads and desserts. The chef taught me to always take time to clear my work station, even during the busy periods. That lesson has stayed with me over the years, and I still don't think I have absorbed it fully. Our first impulse when things get busy is to frantically sling things around, but this is ultimately less efficient. It takes more presence of mind to do things with intention, but it saves time and energy over the long run.

Do you have a tendency to take shortcuts? Name three ways that you try to take the easy way out. See if this tendency does not cause more problems, as things have to be redone and apologies have to be made. Examine also the emotional states associated with the frantic behavior, which can be similar to the feelings behind procrastination.

Beyond Advantage and Disadvantage

I plan for the future based on what makes me and those I love feel whole and well. I let go of money and privilege as the measures of all worth.

We have been conditioned by society to view life like a game of Chutes and Ladders. We view every decision in the light of whether it enhances or subtracts from power and prestige, social status and economic advantage. But a ladder that leads to less life satisfaction is not worth climbing, and sometimes going down a chute can lead to happiness and spontaneity. In reality, life is chaotic, and no one can tell you what will bring you joy. We all just have to improvise, to make a free choice and accept the consequences, good or bad.

You may be facing a big or small life decision today. Increasing the pressure on yourself will not help. Think instead that either way you go, good things await you on the other side. Deeply sense the universe as a loving and supportive place that will make good on all of your decisions. Picture yourself being safe and secure throughout all of your days.

The Transparent Envelope
of the Present

I acknowledge that I do not have strict privacy, as everything that I do or think affects all beings born. Time folds inward around this moment, and this time and place affects all times and places.

The past may be the past, but it is still very much with us. Because all things are interrelated, each and every action puts its impress on the web of connections that make up the universe. For that reason, past, present, and future are inextricably bound with one another, so that it scarcely makes sense to think of them as separate. Action applies to thoughts, words, and deeds, and the implications of each and every action ripple outward until all of the force behind the action has been exhausted. We can do nothing on a purely local or private level, because we are all bound together in the same networks of causation.

As you settle into your meditative state, see yourself as completely transparent, your thoughts, intentions, and emotions on display for all to see. Let go of the notion of a zone of privacy, of an interior space. Rather than letting this idea scare you, open yourself to this new way of looking at things.

Oscillation and Interconnection

I recognize my mind and body as arising from a series of nested processes.
I cannot say where I begin and nature ends.

Wave forms can be used to describe many phenomena in nature, from music to gravity to brain states. Oscillation describes reality more fundamentally than the idea of atomic, separate entities. To be sure, we can still think in object-oriented ways, but we should remember that the objective point of view is partial and provisional. The connections between things matter every bit as much as their uniqueness and separateness, and what we consider to be static objects are actually quite active and ephemeral.

As your inner dialogue occurs, trace these thoughts to the source. See if you can unwind the chain link by link. Keep the questioning attitude open as long as you can. Stay with the question of how and why your consciousness arises.

Disarming Self-Criticism

I look beyond the immediate criticism to the larger issues at hand.
I see how I am involved in networks beyond myself, and I surrender the sense
that everything depends upon me.

The self-critical or self-deprecating attitude paradoxically arises from an overdetermined sense of self. The world does not hinge on my sins of omission or commission. I am as important as any other being, but no more. And what I call myself is not a thing or person but many smaller agencies, many fluid processes. The person or self must disappear so that I can see my inclusion in the larger cycles of nature.

Perhaps you have some persistent self-criticisms. During your meditation, see that the trait that bothers you depends upon other traits, which, in turn, are affected by conditions outside themselves. Turn your attention from only seeing the flaw to seeing the entire system that supports it. Then you may be able to more effectively address the perceived problem.

A Flexible Sense of Self

I do not predetermine my capabilities, but I allow them to expand naturally according to the challenges that arise in my life.

You can do much more than you think you can do, handle much more than you think you can handle. Do not turn down an opportunity simply because of the fear that comes from a new challenge. When you make yourself available for something new, your capacities expand in order to incorporate the unfamiliar activity. Your self-definition must be flexible enough to make room for the new, so that you rise to challenges rather than shrinking from them.

What would you love to do but are afraid to do? Can you push just a little closer to that fear? Can you expand your capacities by just the tiniest amount? Put all of your energies into growth and expansion. What you set into motion within the space of meditation becomes reality in the fullness of time.

The Best-Laid Plans

I plan my affairs in such a way as to avoid the extremes
of well-intentioned neglect and obsessive control.
I express my care through an appropriate level of attention to detail.

Why do good plans, carefully executed, still fail? The answer to that unanswerable question must have something to do with change, the shifting, unpredictable nature of our interdependent universe. When a project makes its way off paper and into execution, the exact nature of the assumptions built into the plan are exposed to the light of day. The closer those assumptions come to an approximation of reality, the more likely it becomes that the plan will succeed. But things change, and people change.

Are you more of a fly-by-the-seat-of-your-pants person or a plan-everything-in-fifteen-minute-increments person? Neither approach is right or wrong, and both have upsides and downsides. Notice your reactions to these tropes. You may find yourself judging people who have a different approach to life. See if you can let go of some of that judgment and learn to enjoy life in your own way while working with others who may not share the same point of view.

Solitude and Community

I notice as I engage with people or shy away from people. I notice my need for alone time and my need for people time. I can be with myself while alone, while spending time in nature, or in a crowd of people.

We are taught through pop psychology that we are either introverts or extroverts, or, in the older vernacular, either shy or social persons. Most of us probably fall somewhere in between, happy to have some quiet time, drinking a cup of coffee and reading a book, and happy to go to the party and socialize with friends. We all have limits and boundaries that may be self-imposed but can still be very powerful. Most important to the practice of mindfulness is to notice where you fall on that spectrum and to observe your thought processes around social interaction. Then any necessary change can happen naturally and not be forced into place.

As you settle into the warm, inviting space of meditation, come home to yourself. Here, in this space, there are no judgments, and you can be entirely yourself. As you withhold judgment from yourself, extend that same kindness to all beings. As you become more open to knowing yourself, you also become more open to others. You can be with others and have them be with you, without all of the grasping and criticizing behavior that leads to a breakdown of trust.

The Luxury of Mindfulness

*I give myself the gift of time, these treasured moments
of stillness in the middle of the day.*

There is an unfortunate association of mindfulness and meditation with a certain preachy tone, a kind of eat-your-vegetables should-ness. That only leads to feelings of guilt and anxiety, the undesirable states that meditation is meant to alleviate. Rather than thinking of meditation as that thing that you know you should be doing, try thinking of it as a luxury, one of the simple pleasures that you afford yourself in life. Think of the velvety folds of your own interior states in the same way that you would consider a fine glass of wine or a piece of really good chocolate.

You may only have a few minutes of quiet contemplation today, but let that be enough. Cherish the time that you do have rather than castigating yourself for not having more. Cherish these minutes and seconds. See them like grains of sand, falling through your fingers, but love every second. Become more present, more grateful, more alive with each passing second. You need not be bound by the past. Now you are free.

Calming That Panicked Feeling

The swans of the vital breath lead my heart to tranquility.
By taming my breathing, I tame the unruly mind.

Emotions have value: they can bring you closer to other people, help you to detect injustices, and lead you more deeply toward your heart's desire. But when emotions become panicked, they lose their function as truth-detectors and have a deleterious effect on health and well-being. When that frantic feeling comes along, still it by means of the breath. Taking long, slow, deep breaths manually intervenes in the connections between the brain, the heart, and the lungs, slowing down the production of stress hormones and restoring equilibrium.

As you look at your life in this sacred space, you may see places in your life that cause stress and anxiety. While observing these turbulent thoughts and emotions, breathe deeply into the difficulty. Expand your breathing to include the belly, the side ribs, and the chest. Inhale sharply for four counts, hold for sixteen, and exhale for eight. After four rounds like this, go into an even rhythm of deep breathing, where the inhalation is equal to the exhalation.

Doing It Now

I will not squander this day, this hour, this minute. I will make the most of the time, for the garment of destiny is woven from these fleeting moments.

Time has a squirrelly habit of getting away from us, so we must make the most of it by getting at least a small piece of what we want today. Think about the major league hitter going up to bat. If he can't get a home run, he'll settle for getting on base. If he can't get on base, he'll settle for staying alive by hitting foul balls. If he can't hit foul balls, he'll at least swing with all his might. Each one of us has been given one more chance today. There is no shame in failure, so long as we get out there and make the most of the time.

Look out upon your mental landscape today. Do you see some hesitation there, some reluctance to give your utmost to life? That sense of doubt or fear, that lingering feeling that portrays itself as your protector, actually hinders you from living to the fullest. With the mighty sound of the *aum*, reduce this negative thinking to ashes.

Cutting Through Confusion and Wavering

I renounce halfhearted attempts and half measures. I commit myself fully to my highest vision, and I live my life as an expression of belief in my cause.

Fight confusion and wavering every step of the way, as this divided mind will nearly always prevent you from achieving what you want. If you want to do something—in business, in spirituality, in sports, in the arts—do it with your whole self. As soon as you get all the way on board with your own idea, plans begin to fall into place, and other people begin to believe in your vision as well. But if you aren't willing to put your toe into the water of the unfamiliar and new, no one else will be willing either. Success begins with a firm determination to see the process through to the end.

Are you living halfway, only committing partway to your vision? In your heart and mind, see your innate power to overcome obstacles. See through the illusion of yourself as weak and afraid. Destroy the self-deprecating thoughts with the increate light of divine consciousness. Feel a great wellspring of power from the heart of the universe, which is no different from your own heart, coming to the aid of your cause. When you wed yourself to this divine potential, great transformations happen.

Out of Despair

In the darkest times, I think of my own small lights.
I find the things that give me joy in everyday life.

No matter how poor your health, how empty your bank account, how low your spirits, life is not over until you decide that it is over. No one can force you to lose your spirits, to wallow in despair, to bow your head in resignation. It is true that our minds and bodies degrade over time, but we can set a watch over our hearts. We can vigilantly refuse to lose faith in ourselves, in our communities, in our ideals. The path out of despair can be very difficult, but it begins with the simple choice to live, to keep going.

If you are feeling despair today, you don't need some master plan for life. Try thinking of a few things that make life worth living. It can be something small, like reading your favorite book or going to your favorite park or taking care of an animal. You don't even need to worry about tomorrow. Think about what keeps you going today.

Begin Again

Whatever happens, nothing is ever final.
The world is reborn with every moment.

I am thinking of a children's song with the repetitive lyrics, "Poor old Michael Finnegan, begin again." But maybe Michael actually had quite a lot of luck, for getting so many chances to start over again. And all of us are lucky too; for each time something bad happens, we get to start over. Sometimes the renewal comes in the form of new material circumstances, but it may also just be a change in disposition. The same event, viewed from a slightly different angle, can be either a catastrophe or a gift, or sometimes a little of both.

Maybe you woke up today on the wrong side of the bed. Feel that frustration now, in your chest or in your head, a cramped, tense feeling. Breathing deeply and straightening your spine, set aside the uncomfortable thoughts and feelings. Breathe into the possibility of a new feeling and direction, something light, peaceful, and satisfying.

Touchstones for Peace

I surround myself with the sights, sounds, and smells that bring me peace.

My grandmother kept a collection of souvenir spoons from each place she visited. She had ceramic figurines of all descriptions, candy jars on every end table and coffee table. She had a fondness for playing various sweepstakes and contests. Certain things will always remind me of her, of the atmosphere of her home. In the same way, I know certain things and places will put me into a peaceful frame of mind: going to the mountains, saying certain mantras, smelling sandalwood. The mind has touchstones that connect it to corresponding moods.

Think now of the sights, sounds, and smells that lead you to a peaceful frame of mind. Make your imaginings as vivid as possible. Capture that mood and stay there as long as possible. Then make it your mission to put more things in your life that give you peace.

States of Mind

*By doing the inner work of mindfulness,
I make my inner disposition align more closely with my ideal self.
I untangle the knots of tension and rest in calm abiding.*

The golden hills of California are actually kind of brown. Georgia is known as the Peach State, but South Carolina produces more peaches. New Jersey is known as the Garden State, but it should probably be called the Highway State. What is your mental state now? And how does that match with your advertising, with the way that you think of yourself? Can you bring the real and the ideal closer together?

Mental states are made up of many smaller processes. Whatever you are feeling now, see if you can break it down into its component parts. For feelings of stress, you might notice a slight headache, an elevated heart rate, shallow breathing, and thoughts of deadlines and to-do lists. Each one of those thoughts and sensations can be broken down in turn. Take your mental state and unpack it, loosening and dissolving it. In this way, you create space that will automatically fill with more peaceful, tranquil thoughts and sensations.

Great but Ordinary

I bow before the great teachers who came before me,
but I believe that what was possible for them is possible for me.

We venerate great teachers like the Buddha, Jesus, Ramakrishna, and Shankaracharya, but we should keep in mind that what they taught is available to all of us. When we put great teachers up on a pedestal, it serves as an unconscious defense mechanism against their teachings. If these people were superhuman, that means we don't really have to try to achieve what they did. But if we view them as normal human beings who expressed an innate divinity common to us all, then suddenly we are on the hook to at least try to live into our potential.

No matter how much time has passed, no matter how many opportunities wasted, we can once more put forth the effort to cultivate mindfulness. Pay deep attention now to this moment, to the sights, sounds, and sensations as they present themselves to you. Then pay close attention to the rhythms of your body, your breathing and heartbeat, the rush of blood in your ears. Then watch the thoughts and the emotions as they play before the mind's eye. Hold steadfastly to the calm center, and remain there as long as you can.

Genuine Teachers

I hold to the teachings, but I express them with my individuality intact.
The teachings make me more myself than I have ever been before.

A genuine spiritual teacher does not want to produce mindless automatons in his or her students. A genuine teacher will get the disciple to particularize and individualize the teachings, to tailor those teachings to each unique situation that arises. Similarly, an advanced disciple knows what disciplines will work on what occasions and how to fit the traditions into his or her life. This requires respect for the lineage or tradition of teaching (*paramparā*), but also flexibility and creativity. A positive interplay develops in which teacher and student are mutually enriched by the relationship.

You may have had bad experiences with organized religion in the past. Here in this safe, silent space you can release those negative memories as you breathe deeply. If you don't have a tradition or a teacher, let that be okay for now. Listen in the stillness, and hold to an expectant frame of mind. You may not be able to see the whole journey, but the next steps will come to you.

Living with the Consequences

I understand that every action that I take has consequences, and I work proactively to leave my future self in a better position than I am in today.

A rubber band, when stretched to its maximum extent, will either break or snap back down to size. This is like the law of karma, which says that no one can escape from the natural consequences of an action, no matter how small. This is a completely natural law pervading the universe, and we don't have to make it superstitious or paranormal in order to understand it. Given that this is the case, that we must live with the choices that we make, let's have them be good choices. Let's pour all of our thoughts and actions into making the world a better place for ourselves and future generations.

Today you may be feeling the harsh aftereffects of decisions you made long ago. Rather than feeling bitter and regretful, cultivate an attitude of acceptance for the consequences of your own actions. If you have already reached a place of acceptance, try to move into a place of gratitude. As you become less resentful, more opportunities will begin to open to you.

The Fake World

I wean my mind from the false promises of our time.
I see through the veil of lies and cling to what I truly love.

We live in a fake world most of the time: the empty promises of politicians, the vapid superficiality of advertising, the incessant gossip of social media. People desperately crave something real in their lives, something that won't let them down. Mindfulness doesn't actually provide any answers. It can't tell you what to do, but it does sharpen powers of observation. Mindfulness makes it easier to spot the games that we play with ourselves and the tricks that other people try to pull on us.

Today you may be feeling weary of all of the cheap and easy solutions foisted on you. Sit here for a few minutes, and do not solve any problems. Do not think about buying this or that. Improve nothing and contribute nothing other than just paying attention to what happens in this space. Maybe you don't get anything out of this time. But isn't that just the point, that we shouldn't be conditioned to expect some quick payoff for our time?

For the Good of All

I cultivate silent resolve within myself to work for a better world. I cast aside cynicism and doubt, and I begin quietly working for transformation.

The situation of humanity on the planet could not be more precarious. Our ecocidal civilizations are on the brink of tipping points that could destroy the life support systems on which all living things depend. We really could lose our clean air and drinking water, our arable land, our social stability. In order for humanity to have a chance, we have to return to a sense of the sacred value of the earth, of interconnection with nature. We must once again value natural beauty and the right of all beings to the means of life.

In the stillness of this hour, pledge yourself to working for the good of all beings, human and nonhuman. Pledge your life and labor for the healing of the earth, for just relations between nations, for a better life for all creatures. Feel this vow penetrating your entire being, growing stronger within you and radiating outward into everything that you do.

Cultivating Contentment

I do not confuse my net worth with my true worth.
I practice contentment in all circumstances.

We have been conditioned to believe that whatever makes the most money is also the most practical course of action. But money produces false valuations, imaginary notions of worth tied to nothing but thin air. Believing in money requires just as much faith as believing in God or Santa Claus. Money in itself is not evil: it is just based on the wisdom of crowds. Crowds can be smart sometimes, but they can also be cruel, capricious, vindictive, and wrong. We have to practice suspicion and question the wisdom of crowds.

Whether you are rolling in dough or scraping the bottom of the barrel, you can still make it your mission to cultivate contentment. Maybe you don't feel naturally contented now, but just try it for a few minutes. Imagine what it must feel like to be contented, and then steer your thoughts and emotions in that direction. If you can catch a little glimmer of this feeling, magnify it and expand it. Then make the playacting become real.

Releasing Grief

Instead of avoiding the difficult places, I actively observe them.
I live into the pain until it teaches me its lessons.

You set your mind on trying to be more spiritual. This leads to reading holy books, fasting, and meditating, and, in general, trying really hard to be a good person. But then somehow it isn't enough. There is still an empty place inside, a gnawing pain that won't go away. All of the pious behavior doesn't make the pain go away, just as alcohol and drugs also do not make the pain go away. What can actually work is to go straight to the pain and sit with it, just as you would sit with a grieving person. The spiritual practices only work when they help us to get into contact with that deep ache.

Your personal pain may be very obvious right now, or it may be buried deep inside. Go to that place of longing, of sadness, of emptiness, of grief. You don't need to comment on this feeling. You don't need to increase it or decrease it. Just listen to it and sit with it. Acknowledge the feeling and give it space. Don't look for a quick solution, and don't try to make things better.

Overcoming Doubt, Lack, and Limitation

I wait and listen for the new Self now arriving. I open my mind to all possibilities and do not confine myself to narrow understandings.

The basic stance that we take toward life can be either confining or liberating. In order to practice transformation, we have to expand our sense of what is possible. What worked in our lives a week ago or a year ago might not work today. We become slaves to our own past successes as we cling to old patterns of action and belief. Beginning from a place of infinite possibility, we can more easily summon our powers to enact the chosen vision for the future. We must be vigilant, pushing through obstacles and difficulties at every turn.

The biggest enemies lie within. In your meditation today, be on the lookout for thoughts of doubt, lack, and limitation. Allow your vision to expand to encompass all possibilities. Open your mind to the idea that you can let go of your old self and become something as yet unknown. Hear the future beckoning, and know that you have experienced only a fraction of what your life still has to offer. You can and will be more than you are now.

The Possibility of Miracles

I can be free from my prior circumstances. I can live into my deepest vision.
I can live the life of my dreams.

One cannot logically believe in miracles: we have to get in touch with them through the irrational, emotional side of our natures. We have to put logic on hold for a while and hold open a door of sheer possibility. We have to access a kind of absurd tenacity: to believe that things can change for the better in a dramatic and instantaneous fashion. Let this be the moment when eternity erupts into time, when I see myself as I truly am, when my demons are, at last, defeated, when the long struggle for clarity finally ends.

Can you get on board with the miraculous, if only for a few minutes? Open in your heart a door of possibility. Hold nothing back of yourself. Bring your intellect, your emotions, your whole self to bear on this moment. See the door of possibility in front of you. What lies on the other side? Open your heart more and more. Let the wisdom come flowing. You hear a word whispered there on the timeless wind. What is it saying?

Grownup Schmownup

I refuse to live in a grim world of constant complaining. I make life into a game of my own making, and I recover my joy for life.

A certain false narrative about being a grownup suggests that adulthood must be characterized by continual anxiety and stress punctuated by self-medication. Wearing cynicism like a badge of honor has become completely normal, as though there were something naive about being happy. So we guard ourselves all the time, lest someone see the playful and light sides of our nature. Above all, we must appear extremely busy and complain often, for the guards are watching. The guards, of course, are people just like ourselves, who are equally worried about status and conformity.

Think of what you could be if no one were watching, if you could just be yourself all the time. Explore the psychic territory of playfulness, joy, and silliness. Practice smiling as you sit here in meditation. Let your whole body become a smile. This will feel quite strange, as though you were breaking the rules. Carry this playful attitude with you as you leave this place.

Beating the Afternoon Slump

I go easy on my mind and body in times of fatigue.
I recover restfulness instead of pushing past my limits.
My health recovers as I move away from quick fixes.

You may experience a slump in the midafternoon, a tired and lethargic feeling. Before reaching for caffeine and sugar, get up and go for a walk. Have a noncaffeinated drink, like herbal tea. Go easy on yourself if you nod off for a minute or two. Weaning yourself off the sugar and caffeine will lead to better sleep at night in the long run, which will reduce feelings of fatigue. The quick fixes will only exacerbate the problem over time, as your system repeatedly goes on overdrive and then crashes.

As you sit in meditation today, you may feel yourself drawing close to sleep. When that happens, you can open your eyes halfway, to allow more light into your eyes. Or you can practice deep but rapid breathing, which is akin to physical exercise (search online for bhastrika pranayama for more information). The third option is to just go ahead and sleep for a few minutes if you are able. Taking this brief pause will allow you to emerge refreshed and continue with your day.

Natural Creativity

I allow myself outlets for expression,
knowing that I belong to the infinite creativity of the divine mind.

Don't buy into the idea that you are not artistic, that you are not creative. Every human being is part and parcel of the mind of God, part of the infinite creativity of nature. There is no such thing as a person who is not creative. Every person alive should write or paint or draw or sing—something, anything that gives expression to feelings and ideas. The work does not have to be marketable or even have an audience of more than one. If you have to sneak time for art and stash it away in a desk drawer, do that, but don't let yourself get away with not attending to some sort of creative pursuit. You will, quite simply, feel better about life when you engage your creative capacity.

Today, get out a piece of paper and write or draw for at least ten minutes. Start without predetermining a course of action, as though letting your hands just do what they will. Observe the process as it unfolds, and don't worry about making something perfect. Perhaps you learn something important about yourself, and perhaps you don't. Avoid the need to make the experience feel profound in some way.

Avoiding Negative Influences

I govern my own emotional and mental states,
and I do not allow myself to be swayed by the negativity around me.

Ever notice how, when you spend time with someone who is constantly negative and bitter, some of that attitude rubs off on you? And you also cannot help but be positive around certain very wise and generous friends? You can't help but go along with the prevailing mood. When you notice that someone constantly brings you down, put a mental red flag by that person. Minimize contact, and keep it businesslike. Keep a watch over your interactions, and make them firm but positive. The relationship will not be close, but you will preserve your sanity.

As you sit here in the silence, observe the currents of thoughts and emotions: some subtle and some very forceful. Let go of the identification with your thoughts and emotions; stand apart from them and observe. You will also notice corresponding states of the body. Take time to slow the breathing and let go of muscular tension.

Through Difficult Times

I abide in quiet contemplation, through good times and bad.

Our sense of the divine comes and goes. We may feel stuck in mundane details, unable to see the magical, beautiful side of things. In these down times, these difficult times, we have to remember that the mystery is still present. Difficulties are part of the divine unfolding. They scour away self-will and ego, they build our strength, and they create new openings to spirit. The very faithful devotee who stays with the practice in good times and bad will be unstoppable.

As you sit here in the darkness, you may feel no flashes of inspiration, no feelings of elation. Sit here in this quiet darkness, waiting expectantly. Build the quiet faith that a dawning waits for you. Just on the flip side of this ordinary moment lies immeasurable bliss. Even if you cannot feel it now, build in yourself the secure knowledge of its possibility.

Accepting the Real

I know that I must live with the consequences of my own actions. For this reason, I strive to embody the highest principles of which I am capable.

At the end of the day, it doesn't matter what anyone thinks of you or me. Each of us carries the natural outcomes of our own actions. So we should work for that which is most imperishable, strive to realize the divine nature. If we work for fleeting rewards, we will reap fleeting rewards. If we work for the eternal, we will reap eternal fruits. Skepticism does nothing to change this basic reality: we must accept what is real and work from there.

As you examine your life, you may see yourself fixated on short-term, fleeting goals. Instead, encourage your mind to dwell on the highest principles that you can imagine. Cultivate feelings of peace, love, and generosity, to the highest degree possible. Allow this contemplation to realign your goals in life, to stretch your thinking and acting.

Inner Satisfaction

I do not seek my satisfaction in material things, fame, or reputation.
I carry my satisfaction with me at all times,
by seeing the divine in the midst of the everyday.

The trap set for us in life is to want more things, more status, more fame and reputation. None of these desires does any good, as there is no logical stopping point for desire. Even billionaires still want more wealth; even celebrities want more fame. In order to stop the incessant craving, we have to reflect more critically on our situation as finite beings in the midst of the infinite universe. We cannot, by adding more things (or more praise, fame, etc.), satisfy ourselves. If we cannot be satisfied with a little, then we cannot be satisfied with a lot. Contentment has to become a practice, something done deliberately.

Cultivate within yourself the attitude of contentment. Look at who you are, what you have, and be content with everything. Halt the craving attitude, which cannot actually be satisfied. Say to yourself, yes, it is good; I have enough and more than enough. Fullness resides within me: I cannot find it anywhere but here.

Escape from Drudgery

I recover my natural zest for life.
I look past the mundane and into the beauty of this life.

Life can sometimes feel like drudgery, as though there were only an endless stream of chores to be done. Recover your natural ebullience by questioning the thoughts that tell you repeatedly that you have nothing to celebrate, nothing new or exciting in your life. Question also the depressed mood: even though it feels heavy, it is transitory in nature. Concentrate instead on the attitude you would like to manifest, the dynamism and joy that make life livable. Put more vigor and enthusiasm into your work, and watch how you blaze through difficulties.

During this midday pause watch the processes of your body, your circulation and respiration especially. See how the entire universe can be characterized by ceaseless, flowing activity. Rather than holding back in resistance, make your life and consciousness part and parcel of the activity of nature. Join with nature, and allow yourself to participate in the general flow of things. Become light and movable, and your problems will dissolve into the general flux at the heart of reality.

The Vehicle of All Possibility

Knowing that all possibilities reside within the mind,
I direct my thoughts toward peace and tranquility. Learning to master the
mind, I lead my life into fullness and completion.

All possibilities reside within the human mind: the hells are there and the heavens also. There are the infinite reaches of space and the ground beneath our feet. In the mind are name and form and the void also. In the mind are pleasure and delight, self-denial and abstention. The mind races quicker than the fastest vehicle, moving at the slightest direction. The road to ruin and the road to victory lie within the mind. Whoever learns to control the mind can have anything; the person who does not control the mind will certainly be defeated.

Here, in this quiet time, notice how quickly your thoughts respond to suggestion. Like a loyal dog, your mind just wants to be helpful. It will follow any trail that you suggest. Give it the suggestion of peace and tranquility. Ask it to relax in this time, and it will respond. Allow it to create the night sky, with stars all around, and sit there in the vastness of space.

Under Suspension

I allow my mind to move out of its habitual grooves by suspending my belief in the old ways of being. I give myself room to try something genuinely new.

The mind has certain habitual pathways that restrain thought. In order to go down a new path in life, it becomes necessary to move out of the customary thought patterns. Meditation and mindfulness, mantra practice and ritual worship help to move the mind out of its repetitive grooves and into a new pattern, one that is open to the possibility for positive change. This reset happens by putting the old patterns of thought under suspension, to interrupt the habitual ways, if only for a few minutes or a few hours. That little separation gives enough respite for a new pattern to emerge.

As you sit here in the quiet, notice the thoughts. See the ones that arise out of season and out of context, that are not applicable to this present moment. See the familiar grievances arise, the thoughts of enmity that have arisen for you time and time again. As you watch the thoughts emerge, put them under suspension. Do not buy into them, but simply let them float there in the mental space.

Steps to Peace and Productivity

I work this day with firmness of purpose, bringing my heart and mind to bear on all that I do. I cut through distraction and place my steps firmly on the path to peace and productivity.

A cluttered mental life leads to poor performance. In order to secure both peace and productivity, we have to put the cultivation of mindfulness in first place. This is done by punctuating the workday with breaks for meditation. Then we have to eliminate excess "noise," such as the obsessive checking of various websites. This does not mean that we must eschew contact with the world, only that real or virtual interactions must not become an avoidance tactic. Finally, we have to work dynamically at something we truly believe to be important. Without these three elements, the mind becomes clouded, and a tense atmosphere results.

As you pause here in the middle of the day, you may note that you have had a tendency toward distraction. Allow a firm resolve to emerge from your mind and heart that you will set aside distraction and work with purposefulness this day. Feel your concentration becoming strong and one-pointed. Feel your spirit becoming eager and energized.

Integrating Spirituality and Practicality

I bring greater balance and harmony between my spiritual and practical natures. I allow these two sides of myself to be mutually beneficial, creating a positive feedback loop in my life.

In the beginning stages of the spiritual life, we may believe we can either have spiritual bliss or activity in the world. Progress comes only by setting the details of life aside to concentrate on prayer or meditation. This works very well in the beginning, but progress can only be sustained by fully integrating the practical and spiritual sides of our nature. We must practice meditation while also being responsible in career and family. This requires flexibility, patience, self-control, and creativity. We have to make what feel like utterly opposite priorities into mutually reinforcing tendencies.

You may have a feeling today that your life is at odds with your search for inner peace. Do not fear: you have set aside this time just for the purpose of reconnecting with your true nature. As you breathe deeply, feel your body, your heart, and your mind coming into alignment. Allow this place and time to capture your complete and undivided attention. Set aside work for just this brief time, and become completely aware of the inner landscape.

Inner Bliss

I sit in silent communion with my inner divinity.
I still the voices of doubt and distraction, taking refuge within.

The bliss of the inner Self is available to everyone: we just have to stop avoiding it. We spend most of our lives fleeing from solitude, fleeing from inner awareness. We find it most uncomfortable to sit and commune with the inner nature. We introduce complications through excessive intellectualization, through a morass of cravings, through reactive emotions. The inner light only needs calm in order to make itself manifest. Get still enough, and the inner divinity will be obvious, more certain than here is a table and here is a lamp.

As you sit here today, your body may introduce complications: a slight headache, a grumbling stomach, that tricky place in your back. Your mind, too, may complain, saying, "I don't get it" or "Nothing is happening." Through all of these protestations, persevere. Go just a little bit beyond your comfort zone, and risk a little.

The True Meaning of Power

I resolve to stop shrinking from my divine mission. I will become a force for peace and healing in my world. I heal myself so that I might heal others.

We are all vectors for transformation, for the building of a more just and compassionate world, but we often shrink from this divine mission. We tell ourselves that we are powerless and unworthy, but this excuse-making is a manifestation of self-will. The divine process in nature wants us to have all of the power at our disposal, to create harmony between people and between species. Power does not have to be a lording-over; it can be manifested in fostering connections, in defragmenting our world. True divine power is manifested in noble service, not in debasement or egotism. When we use our abilities to help other people or to heal the world, we take part in the divine power at the heart of nature.

Today, cast aside all self-doubt and know, deep down in your heart, that you have the power to transform your life and your world. See there, in the darkness, your innate potential, which longs to burst into the world. You are very talented, intelligent, and strong. You have everything that you need to make your life whole and your world whole. Commit yourself now, in the silence, to the full expression of your innate divinity.

Deep Breathing and Emotional States

When I feel the afflictive emotions, I practice deep breathing
to bring myself into calm. I can learn to modulate my own
emotions through breathing and mindfulness.

The emotions often over-respond to a crisis, amping up feelings of stress and anxiety. Instead of directing focus toward the external threat, the stress response attacks the body itself, leading to reduced sleep and increased inflammation. Meditation offers a drug-free way to decrease negative emotional states, beginning with control of the breath. It is very important in tense situations to increase the length of the breath, to take a complete inhalation and exhalation. This sends the all-is-well signal to the brain, so it slows the production of stress hormones.

Each time when you sit down to meditate, focus on the breathing. Sit up as straight as possible, and then breathe into the three areas of the stomach, the side ribs, and the chest. Even if you don't count the breath, focus on expanding these three areas. You will also note that this deeper breathing supports good posture, as the lungs push against the spine and the chest rises.

Awake and Contented

I move my full attention toward the task at hand.
As I become fully present to my work, I easily move through
difficulties, and the job becomes more pleasurable.

You don't have to master or control your work; you just have to be present to it. As soon as you bring your full self to bear on any given task, the solutions immediately start coming. Creative blocks come from divided attentions, trying to remain distracted but also get work done. Mindfulness has a near-magical power to make the job go quickly and easily. The work also becomes more enjoyable with more attention invested into it. Little details that otherwise would have escaped notice now become important.

You may feel discouraged today at the amount of things you have to do or the perceived tedium of your work. Picture yourself attending fully to the work, moving easily through difficulties, and getting more done than you thought possible. Imagine yourself working without fatigue, mentally awake and emotionally contented.

Unfun but Necessary

I cut straight to the heart of the matter by attending to what needs to be done. I recognize mundane tasks as very important to my spiritual practice. I cannot practice mindfulness without attending to all of the little details of life.

There is a pleasure to be gained from procrastination, a sort of guilty pleasure in doing something fun but not to the point. But there is also a pleasure to be gained in taking care of business, getting things done, and being productive. There is a satisfaction that comes from completing a job, large or small. Sometimes you can trick yourself into doing something unfun but necessary (paying taxes, folding laundry, making spreadsheets) by saying to yourself, "Think of how good it will feel to be done with this." Doing at least one thing a day that is unfun but necessary will speed your progress in life.

Mindfulness does not mean bliss all the time. Sometimes it can mean seeing what needs to be done and doing it in the most efficient manner. Things may be arising in your mind right now that you have left undone. Will yourself to attend to the neglected task, and then redirect your mind to meditation. When you have finished with your practice, begin the neglected duties, starting with the one that is most important for your life's mission.

Working Through Frustrations

I understand that my current frustration doesn't
necessarily mean that I am on the wrong path. I continue
to work diligently, even in the absence of complete understanding.

You will not always be happy with your work. Some days will just be frustrating, and this will be true even if you have the perfect and most meaningful career path. Don't use emotional states as a barometer for how things are going. You may be more effective than you know, and sometimes we break through significant obstacles on the really tough days. Above all, do not make major career decisions in the heat of the moment: take the time to step away and reflect before doing anything drastic. Discern the difference between normal difficulties and existential ones.

Whether you feel like today is going well, or whether today feels dull or stressful, give yourself this break. Take the time now to detach from pressing daily tasks. Set them aside in your mind's eye. Now see the emotions, turbulent or tranquil, and set those aside as well. Take this moment of rest in the quiet darkness of your own body. Dwell here in the darkness, feeling no pressure to have the answers or understand life's problems.

Chosen Divinity

I affirm the validity of spiritual guides, and I let my inspiration take root in my life. I spend some time each day in communion with my chosen divinity.

Let your chosen divinity be your lamp wherever you go. If you don't have a deity or saint to whom you feel attached, keep searching various world philosophies and religions until you find a spiritual or intellectual figure who speaks to you. If you have a guru or teacher, thank your lucky stars, and meditate on that person each and every day. Your devotion to a path, sacred or secular (or some combination thereof) should take you deeper into your own personality, making you more yourself than you were before. Your problems should feel lighter, and inspiration should come more easily.

Form in your mind an image of your chosen inspiration, making your vision as detailed as possible. Then sit there in silent adoration or communion for a few minutes. Sometimes you may feel a conversation emerging with that divine being. If not, that is perfectly okay: don't try to force it. Just spend some time there with your beloved inspiration. Sometimes the wordless states can be even more powerful and moving than trying to force some inner vision or revelation.

Pitfalls and Possibilities

I firmly choose to express the best that I have within me. I commit myself, through concrete action, to healing, to joy, to change. I renounce despair and commit myself to the path of joy and light.

As you look out at the landscape of your life, there are many ways in which you could fall into despair, and there are also many ways in which you can find contentment and bliss. Dynamic action becomes the key factor differentiating the bad outcomes from the good ones. When you face your problems directly and make even the smallest effort at addressing them, things improve, both in the concrete situation and in your internal states. Likewise, when you take full advantage of the opportunities available for you for health and well-being, you will feel so much better than if you were to just lie on the couch and watch television.

As you sit in meditation, the possibilities are arrayed around you. Bring the divine light up the spinal column and through the crown of the head as you breathe deeply. Picture this divine light strengthening the possibilities for positive change and eliminating the pitfalls of depression and despair. Know that you have within you the possibility for a divinely inspired and beautiful life.

This Waking Dream

I let go of my hold on this transitory world, releasing the thoughts that hold me so tightly. I see everything as a manifestation of one overarching reality.

Everything now passing before your eyes is smoke and ashes. Everything passes away, and, for that reason, cannot be grasped and held. Reality is an illusion in the exact same sense that a dream is an illusion: because it ends. You may protest that we can awake from a dream, whereas we cannot awake from what we call normal life. But we do awake from everyday awareness when we realize it as fleeting and transitory. At that moment of awareness we become unburdened from everyday cares and can see things in their totality, as moments or modes of one overarching reality. We can see both ignorance and knowledge as part of one divine will that holds us all in its spell.

In this time of meditation, recognize everything that passes before your mind's eye as fleeting and transitory. Dismiss the thoughts that arise with a strong exhalation, or you may use a word or phrase like "not this" or "release." You may also use the mantra *aum namah shivaya*, which means, "We bow to the consciousness of infinite goodness," or "All of this is part of the divine mind."

Forgiving Yourself

I recognize that change begins within my own heart. I forgive myself for the mistakes that I made in my youth and in my ignorance, and I pledge myself not to self-punishment but to living in a better way.

Freedom begins the moment we stop punishing ourselves for mistakes made in the past. This applies to all areas of life, from finances to relationships to career. When the past loses its hold, we can begin to form new ways of living, which become new habits, which, over time, will lead to a completely new reality. The first step must be self-forgiveness, without which forgiveness for others is impossible. But it can be very difficult to forgive ourselves, especially when we feel we have made major mistakes. The process begins with the simple act of admitting that forgiveness is possible. Then we can speak that forgiveness to ourselves and gradually live into it.

Nothing you have done in the past is ultimately irrevocable. If you have something lingering in your memory that you can't let go, picture a great furnace in the heart center, the breath its bellows. As you breathe deeply, the fire glows white hot. Release the troublesome thoughts and memories into the inner fire, so that they are devoured completely. All you need to find today is the slightest sense of what it would be like to live without regret.

Larger Context

I do not deny the analytic, fact-based nature of my mind, but I place information in its larger context, as part of the natural networks in which humanity is situated. I strive to see the whole picture and not just one locality.

The analytic, active mind excels at examining situations from different angles, weighing the pros and cons, and keeping detailed information. Increasingly the analytic mind partners with technologies like smartphones and computers. But this fact-driven approach does not truly succeed at putting information into its larger context, zooming out to look at the human being situated within the networks of nature. Mindfulness and meditation help with this task of looking at things holistically, taking all of the data points and placing them within a larger frame of reference. This broad-minded style of inquiry is increasingly rare and much needed.

You don't need to deny your fact-based, analytic side in order to practice mindfulness. When the factoids appear before your mind's eye, place them under suspension. Allow the information-based style of thought to remain there. See its findings arrayed before you, but avoid drilling down into any particular vein of inquiry. Strive to remain the observer of all that the mind surveys. Go into a restful, contemplative mode in which the analytic mind rests and the receptive mode takes over.

New Possibilities for Consciousness

When I close my eyes to meditate, I go into the unknown as an adventurer.
I may find unexplored connections, new vistas of awareness.

Formal schools of meditation have existed for thousands of years, since before written language, and yet, in a sense, the science of purposeful awareness remains in its infancy. When you sit down to meditate or practice mindfulness in daily life, you become not just a practitioner of a technique, but also a codiscoverer of new possibilities for consciousness. You may be the person to open new horizons of the spirit, the person to make discoveries that will transform humanity and the earth itself. Mindfulness opens the gateway to new creative possibilities, making possible novel combinations and insights that would not be available within discipline-based, fragmented thought.

Today, if anything appears before your mind's eye that you have seen before, send it away. Tell your mind, "I want to see something entirely new." With time and a lot of practice the mind will comply. When it presents that something new, send this away as well, saying, "I want something better." Repeat this process as long as you are able.

Meditation Journal

I engage in self-reflection on my meditative practice,
always looking to deepen my understanding.

If you haven't begun one already, you may wish to keep a meditation journal. Record the type of practice that you did and any relevant notes. Did you say a mantra or not? Did you engage in any rituals or image-based practices? How long were you able to hold to inner stillness? Did you use breath control or not? Were there favorable or adverse conditions in your surroundings? You want to look for big patterns over time, and, most important, avoid using the journal as a punitive measure against yourself. You may use a code or cipher if you are worried about someone reading it, but don't make the code so difficult that you cannot refer back to it easily.

Sit silently for a period of ten to twenty minutes. Then get out a small notebook or piece of paper and reflect back over the past five to seven days, making an entry for each time you practiced formal or informal meditation. Try to keep this light and easy: you don't want your journaling to become tedious. It should become another tool for self-awareness, a meditation in and of itself.

Between the Thoughts

I examine my mind as a marvelous instrument,
but one that I can nevertheless understand. As I understand the mind better,
I can put it to better use. I become more at ease with
myself and less prone to frustration and anger.

The mind is a very good information-retrieval tool, but that is not its most interesting feature. In meditation, we want to go for the spaces between the thoughts and not the thoughts themselves. We want to become aware of what had previously gone unnoticed, to begin to separate memories from linguistic constructions from emotions, kind of like taking apart an engine and looking at it as a schematic drawing. When we understand better how the mind works, we can set about optimization; or rather, the optimizations come along naturally when we have gained proper understanding. We refrain from doing things that put the mind at odds with itself, that cause mental clutter and confusion.

Today, observe the mental chatter and see how much space you can put into your inner monologue. See if you can go a few seconds without bringing to mind a word or image. Then set about expanding these blank spaces. Don't get frustrated with yourself: treat this as a game in which you have no stake.

Shared Destiny

I affirm my place within the communion of all creatures.
As I free myself from my illusions, I free others as well. I work for the
well-being and growth of all things under heaven.

In mindfulness and meditation the young person has no advantage over the old person, the rich person has no advantage over the poor person, and the educated person has no advantage over the illiterate person. People from all backgrounds and abilities have emotional and mental wrinkles that need to be smoothed, cherished illusions that need to be pierced, doubts and deceptions that need to be overcome. We all partake in the human condition that itself is part of the animal condition, which arises from the larger processes of nature. When we lighten our own burdens, we simultaneously lighten the burdens of others, as we all share a common destiny.

Today is just an ordinary day, but that is also something quite wonderful. As you go into your place of mindfulness, recover a sense of possibility. Today may be the day that you see through the problems that have long plagued you. Today may be the day that you escape longstanding false beliefs. Today may be the day when your burden is lightened. When you leave this place, make sure to share the light with others wherever possible.

The Reservoir of Belief

I constantly reevaluate my worldview to look for beliefs that may get in the way of my unfolding potential. I tailor and adapt my life philosophy to fit with the circumstances of my life at this point in time.

Human society holds a reservoir of beliefs, some outmoded, some false, some useful and good. But the truth value in the abstract doesn't matter very much: what matters is truth value for you at this moment in your life. The ideas that worked for you as a teenager may no longer work today. A belief system that appeals to billions of people may not be inspiring to you. At the same time, you don't need to start all the way from scratch. All we need for an inspired life is to find some perspective that we find inspiring and then adapt it to our particular circumstances. Because those circumstances change, the beliefs will need to change as well. There is nothing hypocritical about changing our worldviews to go along with the stages in life that we happen to be living.

As you survey your thoughts today, you may notice yourself clinging to something that worked well for you at one point in time, but perhaps it no longer does. What would it be like to abandon a belief that no longer suits you, perhaps even one that you consider a core part of your identity? Sometimes more can be gained by subtracting than adding. Are you ready to make the leap into the unknown?

Ready for Change

I am willing to let go of something in order to gain something. I surrender the darker side of my own nature in order to welcome the light now arriving.

Are you ready to give up that pessimistic slant of mind, that gloomy disposition, that dull lethargy? It is perfectly possible to change aspects of our personalities that may have been in place for decades, but we first have to be willing to do the work, to say yes to the possibility of change. We have to renounce whatever hidden benefits we received from the old trait and also embrace the positives and negatives of the new trait that we would like to adopt. Then we have to work very diligently for a long time to replace old habits with new ones, so that they become automatic parts of our natures.

For your meditation today, look for mental complaints that may arise. Take the complaint and rephrase it so that it becomes a word of thanks. This will feel extremely odd. For the rest of the day, and perhaps longer, resolve to not complain about a single thing. You may find yourself making mistakes, but persist in the practice anyway. This one practice will make a big difference in your life.

Unscreened Life

I take a break from virtual reality and return to the actual world.
I strive to maintain a connection with those around me and
avoid escaping into digital fabrications.

Think about the word "screen." Our worlds are filled with screens these days: televisions, laptops, tablets, and smartphones. And yet "to screen" also means to filter or to deflect. Looking at a screen means keeping the rest of the world at bay. Staring at a screen all day is rather like walking around with a fishbowl on your head—you get a great view of the world inside of the bowl, not such a good view of the world beyond. Somehow we have to stop looking at reality through the screen, to get back to the world as it is. I don't think cold turkey will work at this point: we have to start with reducing the amount of screen time every day.

Take a few hours today to go offline and live in an analog fashion. Read a paper book and write with a pen or pencil. Don't escape from conversations by pulling out the smartphone. See how long you can go without your electronic pacifier. Notice the feelings that go along with cutting yourself off from digitalia: the fear of missing out, even a sense of guilt. Find a few occasions during the day when you can connect with someone face to face.

Dialogue, Not Monologue

I accept that I must sometimes yield to the forces in my path. I practice flexibility and surrender, and, in this way, I find self-expression and growth.

Much of our frustration in life stems from trying to impose a desired ordering on the world: we have in our heads a certain vision of the way things should be. We forget that the world is under no obligation to conform to our desires, and then we get frustrated when the plan doesn't seem to be working. The world pushes back against our desires, but this does not have to be viewed as negative or oppressive. Each obstacle that we encounter presents an opportunity for flexibility and reevaluation, a chance to refine our vision and work on ourselves. In this back-and-forth with the world, we become more than we ever knew we could become.

Today, you may have certain areas in your life in which the world is pushing back against your plans. Rather than trying to force things to work the way that you imagined, can you give a little? Concentrate for a few minutes on bending rather than breaking, fluidity rather than rigidity. If you allow yourself to embrace the attitude of flexibility, you may see some solution to your problem.

Acquaintance with the Shadow Side

I get to know myself as much as possible, even those unflattering parts of my personality that I would rather not see. I prepare myself in advance for the troubling situations that will inevitably arise in my life.

Become deeply acquainted with your shadow side, with the triggers in your life that make you angry, depressed, and anxious. Know, in great detail, the typical scenarios that cause you to lose your calm and go into panic mode. Maybe it's an overdue bill, an annoying coworker, a health issue, or a relationship problem. This situation has likely arisen many times in the past, and it will arise again. The situation arises as part of your karmic training, and it will persist until you learn the lesson that it is trying to teach you.

Picture one such scenario right now, a situation that would normally cause you to lose your cool. Now, picturing the scenario vividly, practice deep breathing and abiding calm. Imagine what it would be like for that situation to arise without causing you emotional upset. Imagine yourself inserting a pause between the aggravating situation and your reaction. Picture yourself dealing with the situation calmly and constructively. Repeat this exercise for all of the troubling areas in your life.

Deliberate Simplicity

I look at the role that I play in diverting myself from my highest path. I stare down my own avoidance tactics. As soon as I set aside distraction and avoidance, I proceed down the path by leaps and bounds.

At the heart of any obstacle in life lies avoidance behavior. You know what you should be doing, but you are not doing it. Why not? Because you have introduced complications in your own mind to keep you from doing what you know would be better. Chances are you have introduced distractions and complications to divert attention away from the problem. Until you can admit your own role in creating these needless complications, you will not be able to proceed down the desired path. If you can admit that you can sometimes be your worst enemy, then you can see a realistic way forward. The illusion lies in thinking that there are these external obstacles in the way, when, in fact, you have fabricated them yourself.

Don't make it complicated. Sit and listen. That's it. Sit and listen. Your mind will crave content, crave instruction, crave X, Y, and Z. Sit and listen. The doing is the technique. The technique is the doing. Sit and realize.

The Eternal and the Everyday

I do not seek to escape into another world: I seek entrance into this world in front of me. I only want to know this: the true nature of what stares me in the face. I ask for and await the deeper sight.

We have to avoid using spirituality and mysticism as another avoidance tactic: our societies are already largely based around distraction as a way of life. We have to keep doing normal, grownup things—paying bills, taking care of children, going to work—while at the same time acknowledging and welcoming the *dharma*, the depth dimension, of everyday life. This deep, divine reality is ever present, and yet we work hard to keep it at arm's length. And then we wonder why we feel sad and depleted. Somehow we have to hold together a sense of the eternal with the concerns of practical, ordinary life.

When you sit and breathe, avoid thinking of a higher, separate reality that you must reach through meditation. Beginning from the presupposition of duality, duality will remain. Think instead of tuning more deeply into that which is already present. Become more perceptive, more alive and alert. Cherish each moment as invaluable.

Back to the Present

I gently lead my mind away from distraction and into focus on this present moment. I put aside the many paths of escape and center myself in these quiet moments.

Think of the vast expenditures that we put into keeping ourselves entertained instead of enjoying stillness. We think that we need high-speed Internet at every moment of the day, as though the world would implode if we did not have access to *YouTube* for four seconds. And then consider the aisles of the average grocery store. How many different versions of processed cheese food do we really need? It's about escape, about distraction, not nourishment. But it's one thing to notice this—which is actually pretty easy to do—and another thing to live in some kind of alternative.

Today, your mind will want to escape so badly, to avoid this reality, which it slanders as boring, mundane, trivial, etc. Gently lead the mind back to present awareness. Coax the mind into perceiving the beauty and wonder in everyday life. Be persistent in leading the mind back to the present, as though you were leading a small, timid animal to water.

Extending Meditation Throughout the Day

I expand the mindful state beyond the periods set aside for meditation.
I take refuge in the calm center of my being wherever I go.

You may notice that you have a wonderful, peaceful feeling when doing seated meditation or puja practice (ritual offerings), but that you quickly lose the thread of devotional feelings when going back to regular work. It is as though your mind quickly snaps back into its familiar routine. In order to extend the meditative feeling throughout the day, it will be necessary to insert pauses at midday and in evening. Beyond that, it will be necessary to have micro-pauses every few minutes, for just a few seconds to recenter and come back to the heart center. You may say a formal mantra or just say something to yourself like, "I am busy and working, but I return to the peaceful center of my being."

If you are able, as you come to this time of reflection, give yourself a brief scalp massage. Then rub your temples, the arches of your brows, and your neck and face muscles. Do a brief meditation while concentrating on the point between the brows. If you have trouble focusing, apply a little Tiger Balm or essential oil to the skin between the brows. This little tingling spot will provide a sensory reminder to focus on that point.

Your Imperfect Gifts

I release myself from visions of perfection,
bringing spirituality into my flawed and broken life.
I let divinity shine through all of my faults and flaws.

In order to succeed in meditation, you don't need to completely eliminate desire. You just need to reduce it so that the light can shine. You don't need to have perfect philosophical understanding: you just need to get close enough so that ignorance does not stop you. You don't need to have iron discipline: you just need a modicum, so that you set aside lesser priorities for a time. Whatever good qualities you have, they are enough to get started. Do not let a false idea of perfection get in the way of your practice. If you learn to understand the workings of the mind, everything else will be attained.

You may have in your head an ideal of the spiritual life, a vision of perfection. There is nothing wrong with having aspirations, but see what you can do right now, in this time and place, to find peace and tranquility. Sitting here in this less-than-perfect atmosphere, with your less-than-perfect psychology, begin focusing on peace. Insist on peace, breathe into peace, and live into peace.

For Good or Ill

I make the reality in which I live, but I also bring others along with me.
I cultivate kindness so that the world might become a better place.

We are all quite magical, godlike beings, only we don't see this part of ourselves. We can make the world into a beautiful, loving, and harmonious place, or we can make it full of greed, anger, and delusion. We really can choose the reality in which we live, and we carry the vibrations of that reality with us in our interactions. We can uplift others, or we can drag them down. We can squash dreams, or we can build them. It all comes down to a choice that we have to make each moment, for good or ill.

As you sit here in this place, think of all of the frustrations in your life right now. Do not flee from them, but hold them in a loving embrace. Fill your heart and mind with the light of love, and will that it should become more manifest in your everyday life. Stay here in this place of inner light and love. When you leave this place, resolve to be a little less guarded, a little more bold in your loving.

A Recipe

I take everything that arises in my environment, and I use those appearances as the raw material for the cultivation of consciousness. I deliberately appreciate the good and bad things in life. I maintain the possibility for clarity at all times, in all situations.

Mindfulness is one part dog slobber, one part sunshine, one part azalea flowers. Add to that a dash of river sand, two dandelions, three pebbles, a silver dime, and a few acorns. Mix well. Let stand, and mix again. Wait for the batter to rise: it will be lumpy. Preheat the kiln of the heart to 108 degrees. Bake the loaf evenly throughout. Divide into equal portions. Feed to birds and squirrels. Distribute the remainder to family, friends, and total strangers. Discard leftovers and bake it again tomorrow, making substitutions as necessary.

Any conditions whatsoever can give rise to mindfulness. Take your situation today, this place and time, and cultivate awareness. Pay attention to what arises, internally and externally, keeping in mind that the inside and the outside are not opposites but feed into one another. As you make your inner states more subtle and responsive, you will be able to perceive the world more clearly. Clarity within leads to clarity without.

Dealing with Doubt

I acknowledge that not everyone will get on board with my practice of meditation. I do not need everyone in my life to go along. I persist through all doubt, making way for peace as I go.

You will encounter people who think that mindfulness and meditation is a ridiculous waste of time. That's okay: do not attempt to proselytize or convince. People come to the practice sooner or later. It is easy to scoff when things are going well, when sensory pleasures abound. The dry times, the difficult and turbulent times, naturally lead to introspection, to a search for a better way of life. Let your practice be your practice, and leave other people to their own journeys, knowing at the same time that we all belong to each other.

You may be harboring some skeptical thoughts today, believing that you are wasting your time here by sitting in silence. Let the doubt hover there in your mind, but without commenting on it or entertaining it further. Go back to awareness of the inner space, of the breathing and the rhythms of the body. The doubt will disappear by itself if you do not continue to support it.

The Search for Dharma

My understanding is not perfect, but I have more than enough
understanding to get started. I know the way with my whole self,
and I put my mind and heart into the search for the path.

Dharma is the way of nature. It is also the right thing to do, right conduct. Dharma is reverence for the devas, which we can call gods or consider to be the depth dimensions of nature. Dharma is also reverence for our teachers and ancestors. As soon as we ask, "What is dharma?" we already begin to practice it. One person who sincerely seeks to understand the dharma is better than a thousand people who are sure that they have found it. One person who practices the dharma absorbs the sins of a thousand people who disregard it.

Today, turn within and ask yourself what the dharma means for you. Another way of approaching this question is to ask what makes you feel whole and at peace and what makes you feel conflicted and miserable. Of course that word "feeling" can be misleading. We have to take a step back from the feelings, not to disregard them but to ask what gives rise to them. They signal some unresolved conflict, something left unnoticed.

Mindfulness While Driving

I practice mindfulness in all areas of my life.
I make the best use of the time, moving deeper into the present reality.

Suppose someone cuts me off in traffic. Before getting angry, I should ask myself, "Can I honestly say that I have never done the exact same thing?" I am not different from the person in the other car. We are two different modes or aspects of the same person, two different characters in the same dream. We should think, "I have been there" or "I will be there" or "That person is me." We should also think about how it feels to be stressed and in a hurry, and then we should feel compassion for that person. This attitude must be cultivated: it will not happen if we just blindly follow the aggressive aspects of our nature. We have all been down the road of anger, we know where it leads, and we know from experience it is not pleasant.

Today, practice mindfulness wherever you go: in the car, in the store, in the workplace. People may notice a change in you, or they may not. But you will feel different—more alive, more peaceful, and more alert. You may lose your focus from time to time, but do not worry. Just go back to paying attention.

Unplugging

I take note of my relationship with technology,
and I moderate my use of media. I participate in virtual worlds,
but I also value the world right in front of me.

Do you control your electronic device, or does it control you? Can you put down your phone for an hour without looking at it? Do you have to respond to every little alert? If you are paying constant attention to your electronic device, you are ignoring large portions of your actual life. You are probably not engaging fully in conversations with colleagues and loved ones, and people probably notice. The quality of your work is likely suffering. You are putting your safety and the safety of others in danger if you are looking at your phone while driving. Start weaning yourself off the device today.

Today, try taking your phone off your physical person for a few hours. Put it somewhere else in the home or workplace, where it will be out of arm's length. As you sit in meditation, you may feel the familiar twitch that urges you to check social media or your favorite websites. Just observe the twitch without needing to comply with it.

Guiding Spirits

I affirm the existence of a subtle world parallel to visible reality. I may find myself among spirit guides, but I do not fixate on contacting them.

I once met an elderly monk with decades of practice in contemplative prayer. He conversed daily with his guardian angel, and he experienced this spirit as giving him helpful advice, showing insights into the scriptures, or guiding him more deeply into his prayers. As you continue in the practice over the years, you may experience just such a guiding spirit, whether or not you want to call it an angel. Just don't force it to happen: invite the presence of such a being but do not force it to interact with you or engage in fantasy behavior.

You may experience something like an aura, the energetic field of your subtle body, when you close your eyes to meditate. It extends out from your body by several feet. Other spirits may hover around your aura, like smaller lights adjacent to your own energetic field. You may come to sense whether these spirits are good, bad, or indifferent. They are generally nothing to worry about, as your cultivation of the inner light will protect you. Even what may appear as monsters or spooks sometimes have more of a trickster nature than actual malevolence. Unless you feel strongly like you are to receive some sort of message, just treat them as you would any other kind of background noise.

Taking a Retreat

When I feel overstressed and need a break, I intentionally ask for rest and renewal. Relief quickly comes my way, and I am able to get away for a few days.

You may feel the lure of spiritual things calling to you, and yet you also have a lot of pressing material work that occupies your attention. Go before your chosen divinity or other sacred figure, such as the Buddha, your spiritual teacher, or so forth and sit for a period of silent meditation. Then ask there before the image to be given a period of retreat lasting a few days. Keep up this pattern for three, nine, or twenty-seven days. You will know inwardly when your request has been heard and when it has been granted. The opportunity will soon arise for you to take the retreat, but it may also require some planning and work on your part.

Whether you are sitting to meditate for a few minutes or a few days, something will always arise at the last minute to pull you away from your spiritual practice. Perhaps this is happening to you now, something pressing that you feel you simply must address. Be vigilant and hold to the practice; it can wait.

Spirituality of Gender and Sexuality

I use meditation as a tool to explore my gender and sexuality. I am open to changing my individual expression so that my spiritual development can proceed.

Gender identity and sexual identity are not separate from spiritual practice. It will be difficult to move deeper into spirituality if something about gender expression does not feel authentic. An excessively rigid gender identity can keep you from developing spiritually. Stereotypically masculine types may feel that yoga and meditation are too effeminate, while traditionally feminine women may feel selfish when tending to inner well-being. The cisgendered (gender identity that corresponds to birth sex), heterosexual script says that men should be strong and impervious, while women should spend all of their time taking care of others. Neither of these typical gender expressions is very conducive to the inner work.

When you close your eyes to meditate, your gender expression may feel more fluid over time. It is not uncommon for men to feel softer and more emotional, while women may become more aware of gender-based trauma. Today, see if you feel differently in the meditative state than you do in your normal, waking state. You may feel led to make some changes. The changes don't have to lead to a full-blown transition, although that happens in some cases, but you may decide to make a few adjustments to your gender presentation here and there.

No Winners or Losers

I release the need to compare myself, favorably or unfavorably, to those around me. I affirm the inherent worth of all beings.

Mindfulness requires getting out of the competitive game of Western consumer societies. We have to stop thinking in terms of dominance—that we must either beat the other person or be beaten in return, that we must either be better or the other person must be better. We have to replace the competitive, zero-sum ethic with an ethic of mutuality and respect. Our sense of self and personhood must not depend upon denigrating someone else, upon robbing the other person of inherent worth. We must come to respect and value difference without thinking in hierarchical terms. We must decenter the self without negating or harming the self: we should insist on respect for others without self-annihilation.

Imagine for a few minutes what it would be like to live without status symbols, without needing to feel better than anyone else. Imagine what it would be like to treat all people equally. Allow your inner attitude to shift toward this vision of equanimity. Unclench your heart from all feelings of superiority. Sincerely wish and vow for equanimity to take hold in all of your actions and affections.

At the Water's Edge

As I sit beside the water, I release my thoughts into the general flow of things. I become one with the water, and my cares are borne away by the current. I am rested, renewed, and restored by the washing of the water.

Beside a lake or river is a good place to sit and meditate. The glassy surface of the water reminds us to be simple mirrors for nature, without needing to add anything of our own. The flowing nature of water reminds us of the transitory nature of all existence. And, of course, water always flows to the lowest place, reminding us of humility. Finally, water is the foundation for all life: despite its apparent simplicity, we all depend on it. Respect and appreciation for clean water will be one of the most important values of the coming century.

If you are able, get away to a pond, stream, lake, or river today. Picture your cares and worries being carried away with the current. Hear the gentle lapping of waves or the murmur of the stream, and see this as emblematic of the cycles of all of nature. Picture the thoughts coming and going, just like waves. Lose yourself in the flow, and become one with it in your mind's eye. Merge into your surroundings and become just another part of nature.

A Break from the Noise

I periodically give myself a break from the constant noise of the world.
I heighten my senses and my powers of concentration
by reducing the input to my mind.

If you feel like you have reached a plateau in your meditation practice, you may have too much audiovisual stimulation in your life. To counteract this tendency, try giving up all forms of media and entertainment for a few days. This would include printed books and magazines. If you allow yourself anything at all, let it be a few lines of scripture per day. This could be the Upanishads, the Psalms, the Tao Te Ching, the Bhagavad Gita, or the Gospels—but no more than a page per day. Also keep conversation to a minimum, and even keep your surroundings as simple as possible. By the end of this restrictive period, you will find your senses heightened and your ability to concentrate enhanced.

When undertaking any restrictive regimen, you may feel afraid of boredom or be afraid of what you might find there in the stillness. Treasure in your heart a hopeful disposition that the gifts of this silence will be far more than what you sacrifice or eliminate. Do not attempt to think about tomorrow or the next day. Think only of the next few minutes. Resolve to keep your vow for now, only for now.

Positive Thinking versus Positive Action

I do not rely on thought alone to transform my situation.
I am willing to take action steps in order to move my life, slowly but
inexorably, in the direction of my dreams.

The problem with positive thinking is that it often amounts to little more than wishful thinking. There is very little difference between wishing or praying for a million dollars (magical thinking) and imagining that a million dollars will soon arrive (positive thinking or manifesting). Better to start small, to think of a few things that you can do today or this week to improve your lot, whether your goal has to do with finances, relationships, or spirituality. Thoughts certainly have power, but the power is much greater when combined with action.

You may have tried some new age techniques in the past and been disappointed. Today, give yourself the chance to begin again. Think of some goal in life that you would like to pursue, something realistic and achievable. Then think of three small steps that you could take either today or in the next week. Write these steps in your planner calendar or journal, and make sure to complete all three of them. Then you can make another list of three items and continue in this fashion.

Lessons of the Chakra

I acknowledge no straightforward division of opposites. Everything naturally transitions from one state into another, and I allow my mind to expand enough to see the higher unity behind conflict.

One of the weapons associated with Sri Krishna, and with other deities, is the chakra or wheel. The chakra is a spinning weapon made of light. It circles on the blue god's upturned finger. We would do well to learn the lesson of the chakra, the wheel, the circle, the flower, which is also associated with the energy centers in the body. Our Western logic focuses so much on dualistic or dichotomous assumptions: one must either be male or female, something must either be true or false, one must either be liberal or conservative, and so forth. But the chakra suggests that reality flows in circles and does not stand still. Reality is not a succession of points on a line segment. Everything naturally flows into its opposite, and reality continues to spin on the axis of Krishna's finger.

You may catch yourself wanting a stable grounding place, a place where you can put down your foot and say, "I am this" or "This is true." Let go of all surety and see how all things transition and change. See the commonality between the opposites. Even this inner darkness that surrounds you is luminous. The space of purposeful ignorance gives way to knowledge. Your worst enemy is your alternate self.

Overcoming Dualism

I see how the world of thought and the physical world overlap and interconnect. I strive to purify the mind so that my experience of the world also becomes pure. I collect myself on the inside so that my world might be orderly and calm.

We falsely believe in two self-enclosed spheres, that of the world "in here" that comprises the thoughts in my mind, and the world "out there," which we call the material world, the world of things. These two points of view are mutually dependent and cannot be neatly divided. The mind arises from the material brain, which physically interacts with the things we perceive. The concepts that arise in the mind do not sit neatly off to themselves; they return again to the world to structure and shade our experiences.

Notice now that, when you close your eyes, you can make for yourself a representation of the world in which you are sitting. It may be more or less detailed, but you can see the room in which you are sitting in the mind's eye. Zooming farther outward, you can make a representation of the building in which you are sitting, of the city or country where you are sitting, and so forth. The outside world can be contained within the inner space, which expands indefinitely, until it contains all that you know of the universe.

The Translucent Body

I do not pretend to be separate from the rest of the world.
I acknowledge my mind as an extension of nature.
I am a conduit for the universe to understand itself.

We often think that we have inside our heads a certain zone of privacy, where our thoughts and intentions are not known by others. Usually we are far more transparent than we think. The people around us, especially those who are highly empathic or are simply well acquainted with our personalities, can guess pretty accurately how we are feeling or what thoughts might be going through our heads. And most of these thoughts are not especially unique or interesting anyway; they are recycled, like common property belonging to humanity.

As you sit here in meditation, practice long, slow deep breathing for a few minutes. It is not uncommon to become aware of the outlines of the skin at this point, and you may sense your body hairs standing on end. See the outlines of your body becoming transparent, as though an observer in the room with you would be able to see straight through you. You may then feel that the outlines of your body disappear entirely, or that your body is simply a point of reference for perceiving the rest of space. See that whatever arises in meditation is not, strictly speaking, yours. It comes from the world and returns to the world. The world sees itself through you.

Beyond Quick Results

I am willing to wait for something worthwhile. I am willing to put other priorities on hold while I attend to my search for illumination. I tenaciously hold to one-pointed awareness while I await the blessing for which I seek.

We live in a culture where everything is available on demand, either streaming online or shipped to our doorsteps in days from anywhere around the world. The shift to mindfulness and meditation can be difficult, because the results may not be so instantaneous. The expectation of gratifying results may be frustrated as the practice unearths uncomfortable truths about our society and about our inner lives. The journey of discovery does not end in five or ten minutes or even in a few years. We continue to work on ourselves and our lives over the decades.

We are conditioned to expect an end product and to be uncomfortable with process. As you sit today, you may be wanting some sort of completion or finality, an end point to your journey. What would it be like to let go of control, to give yourself to the inner life completely and fully, without regard for the result? Can you abandon yourself a little more today, move a little more deeply into the practice?

Removing the Tarnish

I come back to myself, again and again, through meditation. I bring my mind back to this present moment. Through this simple discipline, the heaviness of existence becomes light.

The word "sin" has so many emotional associations: it feels shameful, dark, and heavy. And it carries a strong risk of abuse, as the priestly powers can use it for manipulation. Think instead of sin being like the tarnish on a piece of silver. Is the silver guilty for having become tarnished? Not at all. The silver is reacting with moisture and pollution in the air to produce that filmy coating. A little polishing restores the luster. What we call sin is really just the outcome of our interactions with the world; it can be removed easily through the practice of spiritual disciplines, which make our spirits bright and shiny.

Today, as you sit here in the silence, remember that the objective is just to come back to yourself, to come back to this present moment. Attention is what is needed, not self-flagellation. The only job that you have is to pay attention for this time set apart. That little effort will be enough and more than enough to transform your life. It really is just that simple.

Training for the Mind

I recognize that having a peaceful life is well worth the effort that it will take to reach a clear state of mind. I am ready and willing to sacrifice my time and energy on a regular basis in order to find the primordial bliss.

A runner who is preparing for a marathon will run hundreds of miles to prepare for that 26.2-mile race. Each week's workout will be planned months in advance to build the proper stamina and speed for race day. It is the same way in meditation and mindfulness. We train each and every day, although we don't really know when the trial will come. Agitation, frustration, annoyance, sadness, anger, depression, or anxiety can strike at any moment. Soon enough, all of the training begins to take effect, and we learn over time to return the mind to a clear, calm state.

As you look at your training regimen, is it so difficult that it comes to feel like drudgery? Or is it so lax that it hardly feels like work at all? You want to be somewhere in the middle, neither too hard nor too easy, while balancing different types of meditation. You want to do some silent sitting, some mantra practice, some ritual worship, some study of scripture, some yoga asanas, and some acts of service. Take the time now to make a plan for your training over the coming weeks.

Releasing the Deepest Self

I let go of the doubts from the past,
and I allow myself to reach my full potential.

As we work on Self-realization, we come to realize just how much our behavior has been characterized by self-criticism and self-blame. We have to learn how to stop castigating ourselves for past mistakes and to learn to take care ourselves along the way, to search for God while also seeking a more authentic personality and better relations with others. The final goal is *moksha*, or release, but there are many intermediate unfoldings, many smaller revelations. The cramped confines of the old self-concept begin to expand as we see the beloved in ourselves and in others. We experience a transformation of aims and objectives along with a gradually shifting personality.

As you sit and close your eyes to meditate, consider yourself as pure, unbounded potential. In this calm space of awareness, release your thoughts about the past. Release self-doubt and self-blame. Release your narrow concept of self. You, in this moment, are entirely free. You don't have to be the person you have always been. If something bothers you, be it in your external conditions or in your personality, you can change it. Picture your heart and mind unfurling, like the fronds of a fern. Make your reality ever more nurturing, ever more loving, and ever more truthful.

Silent Change

I let go of my obsession with progress. I let go of my insatiable desire for results. I sit here, as I am, and allow the inner space to absorb me.

You may feel like nothing has changed since you started meditating. Think about this example. When flying on a plane, you feel like you are stationary, even though you are hurtling along at 30,000 feet above the earth. From your own vantage point, nothing changes, while a person on the ground would see the plane as a streak across the sky. The changes in your life take place all the while, unbeknownst to you. One day you will just find yourself in a completely different place. It is enough to just stay with the practice.

Today, leave aside notions of progress and evolution. Sit here in quiet communion with your own nature. Observe the breath, observe the body, observe the thoughts. Let go of the desire for results. Let go even of the desire for peace and contentment. Sit here, not knowing and not wanting. Take shelter in this inner darkness. Allow the inner space to absorb your body, your thoughts, and your emotions.

True Power

I let go of the need to be recognized for my achievements. I let go of the need to be perceived as successful by others. I seek only union with ultimate reality, and I direct my efforts toward the supreme goal. If others follow, they follow. If they do not, they do not.

We mistake the notion of power as being able to control and manipulate people at will. True power has nothing to do with personal aggrandizement, but stems from the merger of the individual self into the whole. The truly powerful person serves others, inspires others, and leads people down the path of union with the All. A truly powerful person does not need wealth and status to impress others: the true person has natural authority, arising from connection to the source of reality. Such rare people move society invisibly, upholding the world with quiet dignity and devotion. We are all fortunate to meet even one such person in a given lifetime, and more fortunate even still to become one.

Today, as you observe your thoughts, you may see traces of desire for fame and influence, for things and status. Acknowledge these thoughts and do not repress them. Allow them to come into the open, but do not interrogate them or interact with them. Stop lending support to such thoughts, and they will fade naturally.

Shattering the Mold

I look to the places where I have been pressed into a mold not of my own choosing. I explore the maligned parts of myself and balance the contrary forces, making myself whole and well.

Western culture has traditionally regarded nonhuman nature, the physical body, and feminine attributes as belonging to darkness and sinfulness. The awakened spiritual practitioner sees the union of forces labeled as light and darkness, and steers awareness toward that which is traditionally neglected and maligned. We find ourselves and renew our world when we heal these binary divisions. The new person now being born harmonizes and integrates masculinity and femininity, nature and culture, desire and knowledge. This process of merger happens in the anahata, or heart chakra, the focal point for the union of contrary forces.

As you close your eyes to meditate, breathe deeply, bringing awareness down into the chest region. Feel the lungs expanding and contracting. See if you can become aware of your heartbeat and the rushing of blood. Feel the heart region expanding, like a cave or temple in the chest. Set an intention in the heart chakra for the balancing of your nature, for the right amount of assertiveness and the right amount of nurturing. Harmonize the left and right sides of the body. Harmonize the intellect with emotions and desiring. Know that no one part of yourself is superior to any other part. Let go of the need to subdue any part of your nature.

Difficult People

I will not let anyone take me away from my mission of finding peace and abiding joy. I practice compassion toward all, but I may renegotiate the terms of my relationships.

You may have overbearing personalities in your life—parents, a spouse, or friends—who have made it difficult for you to reach your full potential. You may be able to make your life work better without completely cutting off contact with these troublesome types. Find for yourself times and places for privacy, for seclusion. You don't have to be completely open with people who are abusive and damaging, especially if they ridicule your spiritual practices. Keep your secrets where necessary, so that one day you can practice in all openness. The naysayers in life may or may not come along for the ride; you can usually still stay in contact, but the relationship will change.

As you sit here in the still center of your being, perhaps people come to mind who have continually made you frustrated and anxious. Look upon these people with compassion in your mind and heart. Do not wish for them to change or rail against them internally for the way that they exist in the world. Resolve silently to find peace in your life no matter how your crazy-making loved ones may behave.

Your Own Spark

*I do not claim superiority to anyone else in my journey through this world.
I claim no unique access to the truth, no surefire way of avoiding
misfortune. I share a common lot with all beings.*

There is no correct way to move through life, no guarantee of safe passage.
The most straightlaced person has no definitive advantage over the most
reckless. The most staid person and the most artistic share the same condition. The wheel continues to turn: the person who is now at the top will
soon be at the bottom, and vice versa. We cast about looking for consola-
tion, and we can find it only in our common lot. We only need to beware of
thinking ourselves immune from the trials of life: my turn will come soon,
and so will yours. We muster our courage and do the best we can.

You may have spent many years looking for the answer, for the ready-
made solution to the problems of life. Perhaps you have come as close as
you are going to get. Rather than looking for more wisdom, sit here with
the wisdom that you already have. Sit here with the goodness of your own
nature, and with the lessons that life has taught you thus far. Sit here with
your own spark, and fan it into a flame.

Natural Processes

I pay attention to my own interior states, becoming present to my own reality. I allow transformation to arise naturally, rather than trying to force it to happen.

Everything in nature goes through cycles: the seed falls to the earth, germinates, and sprouts. The young plant pushes out of the soil, flowers, and produces its fruit. The cycle repeats itself over and over again. Our lives go through phases just like this. We can't expect to be energized and excited all of the time. We have periods of what feels like stagnation, akin to the fallow ground in a garden. These times have an important function of providing restoration and rest. The cycle begins again soon enough. Before pushing forward in any project, we should pause to be aware of the cycles in process and our current situation within them.

You may have noticed your enthusiasm for meditation waxing and waning. Take a look within yourself. Are you full of fervor and devotion, or do you feel dull and lifeless? Today, work with whatever feeling you have. Notice whatever appears rather than trying to force yourself in a new direction. As you become more present to your own internal states, transformation will happen naturally, almost effortlessly.

Hidden Wisdom

I make way for the infinite wisdom that resides within my heart.
As I clear the inner space, the best part of my nature shines,
and I move through life with intuitive grace.

We all have wisdom hidden within, just ready to serve as a guide in all matters, trivial or profound. The trouble is that we are unable to access this guide, due to emotional and mental turbulence. In order to feel the subtle influence of our own wisdom, we must become still within so as to quell strong emotions and reduce the insistent thoughts. Keep in mind we don't need perfect calm: only enough quiet to allow the inner wisdom to find an opening. Taking a few periods during the day for silent contemplation will be enough to reap the benefits of the inner guide.

Picture your mind like a muddy pond, the sediment swirling all around. As you center yourself in your calm center and feel gravity pulling down on your body, the turbulent thoughts and emotions begin to settle. Inner clarity emerges naturally as these afflictive states begin to subside. Without any conscious effort on your part, solutions arise unbidden. You spontaneously go about your day, and things work a little bit better.

Taking Out the Trash

I do not allow the clutter to accumulate.
I keep my house in order through daily diligence.

Meditation is a chore, like taking out the trash. Imagine if you did not take out the trash for a few days, for a week, for a month. How gross would that be? Meditation is a chore, but that doesn't mean that it has to be difficult or burdensome. It is much easier the more often it enters into our routines, and it can be cheerful and easy. Meditation, whether undertaken formally or informally, clears away all of the mental rubbish and restores internal order. It is such an easy and beneficial thing, and such a kindness to ourselves. It leaves pleasant feelings in its wake, free of charge.

You may have some negative thoughts and feelings bothering you now. To get rid of them, you must pay attention to them, but without encouraging or prolonging them. Watch the internal chatter as it arises, and notice the feelings. Do not engage with the thoughts or add to the internal monologue. Feel any physical or emotional pains that may arise, but do not add any drama to them. Through bare awareness, through sustained inquiry, negative states can be overcome.

Releasing Persistent Guilt and Regret

When I feel hobbled by my past mistakes, I speak forgiveness to myself.
I wait for the day when I will no longer feel bound by choices made long ago.

What do you do when you have a feeling of guilt or regret that won't go away, no matter how hard you try to release it? Some mental states are so persistent that they have to be lived away, endured for some long period of time, perhaps years or decades. That said, every negative state has an expiration date, because thoughts and emotions are ephemeral things. When the right mental discipline combines with the right life conditions, the troublesome mental state will disappear. In the meantime, it will be best to minimize the impact, like a person living with an old injury or a chronic illness.

Speak forgiveness to yourself today, for whatever might be bothering you, perhaps a mistake you feel that you made long ago. Maybe you are still living with the consequences of that decision. Just say, "I forgive you for doing _____." You may not feel any relief today, but if you keep talking to yourself in this kind manner, eventually something will change.

Old Souls

I know that there is more to myself than I can imagine or express.
I carry the aeons with me in my heart of hearts.
I know all beings, and all beings know me.

We are all old souls, with much more depth and many more experiences than we can know consciously. If we could see ourselves in our true natures, we would look like little suns, only more colorful. All of us have been male and female, every plant and animal species, rocks and dirt and dust. We have been many different nationalities and lived in every climate. If we could see clearly, we would have this deep feeling of kinship with every living being. We would feel so much larger than this present lifetime and personality. Each of us struggles to live into our own selves, to be as full and complete as we already are beneath the surface.

You may not believe in reincarnation; if you do not, think of it as a metaphor. Imagine now what it would be like if you had a thousand or a million lifetimes to lead. Imagine all of the places that you could visit and all of the possibilities that you could explore. Now, imagine all of that potentiality coiled tightly within yourself, in a tight little ball of energy. Imagine what it would be like if you could pull on just the right thread to allow all of that potential to be released into the present.

Abiding Peace

I set aside my goals and my vision in order to find tranquility in this less-than-perfect world. I do not make myself crazy by pursuing the unattainable, but I simply do that which is within my power to transform my situation.

We have a tendency to conflate peace and tranquility with material abundance and psychological happiness. But the emotional state of happiness does not last. The kid gets the candy and is happy. Someone takes the candy and the kid is unhappy. In mindfulness practice, we look for something more abiding than getting this or that desire satisfied. We look for a peace that does not depend on favorable conditions; one that can happen whether we think things are going well or badly. This is the peace that comes from acceptance of things as they are, rather than always striving to reach some unattainable goal. We work and exert ourselves as usual, but we detach from the expectation of gain.

Do you have some expected reward hovering just beyond your grasp? Is it having a big retirement fund or a bigger house? Or is it something more spiritual sounding, like volunteering in another country or moving to an ashram? Take a few minutes to honor your goals and intentions while at the same time freeing yourself from their grip. Redirect your mind from product to process, from destination to journey.

Small Hints

I look for the small interventions that change my way of being in the world.
I make small, everyday actions the focus for my mindfulness practice.

We all have to have goals to shape our aspirations and heroes who embody our values. We are project-oriented creatures, which is all well and good. But our goals can sometimes get out of hand, leading us to despise our current reality in favor of the dream out there on the horizon. There is nothing wrong with having a really big vision for the future, but we sometimes have to set aside that vision and focus on more proximate goals, or even change our goals entirely. This process of constant revision is actually different than the usual advice of taking "baby steps" toward our dreams. Sometimes the path is nonlinear, and the desired destination also changes. We wind our way around to the purposeful life, stumbling toward it.

Forget about the really big vision for now. Open yourself to the inner darkness and put yourself into an inquiring attitude. Be willing to set aside your life as you know it now. In the darkness ask for the tiniest suggestion for how you might do something differently or live in a better manner. Resolve to stay here in this darkness until you have received some small hint for personal transformation.

Making Worry Into an Ally

I do not ignore my worries, but I look for the insight that they have to offer.
I take action to keep worry at bay by practicing diligence in my affairs.

Worry can become a friend if it is not allowed to fester. Let your worries become your guides, not your masters. If something worries you, take some small action to placate the worry. You don't need to defeat worry once and for all: just defeat it for the time being. If you are worried about getting into a traffic accident, drive as safely as possible. If you are worried about not having enough money in retirement, formulate a savings plan. If you are worried about a big project, start knocking out parts of it. By converting worry into positive action, you deprive it of its power. A little bit of worry can make you more conscientious, while overwhelming worry can be paralyzing.

Take a look at the things that worry you the most in life. Have you made a concrete plan of action to tackle the worry in question? If you haven't done this, the worry will likely continue to recur until you address the issue. Take a few minutes now to find a few things that you can do to realistically address the disturbing thoughts that have you concerned.

A New Creation

I unleash my mind in new creative dimensions.
I allow myself the freedom to exercise my imagination,
to tackle new problems, and to venture in new directions.

Sometimes life may feel like dull repetition of the same tasks, the same conversations, and the same occurrences. The human mind is meant to exercise its creative capacity, not to just mechanically complete tasks. You must unleash your mind so that it can fathom new directions and new solutions. Otherwise, restlessness leads to frustration, which can lead to haphazard or reckless behavior. Use the mind to invent something, to make something, or to solve something. Don't make the mind into just another machine: let it play. Give it something to do that requires more than just cursory attention.

You may be feeling bored or tired today. Maybe you feel like you have spent years or decades doing the same old thing. As you close your eyes today, slough off those old habits of the mind. See your consciousness expanding into new areas of awareness. See yourself becoming a new person, a new creation, and a creator as well as a creation.

The Big Man Upstairs

I look into my God concepts, seeing if my own distorted sense of divinity may be causing obstacles in my life. I open myself to the many possible faces of God, to the manifoldness of truth as it appears to me.

The problem with the typical Western idea of God is that it fosters a sense of dependence. The deity is normally pictured as a sovereign king, and that automatically implies that the worshipper is a peasant or serf, who can only beg for scraps. This drains humanity of agency and responsibility. We can reclaim the idea of God if we drop the notion that we ourselves are helpless over our fates. All of the medieval notions of God must fade away in favor of a God who resides within nature, not over and above nature. Whether you think of yourself as a theist or an atheist, a pagan or a pantheist, see how damaging it can be to live life in a completely passive, dependent manner. If there is a capital-G God, that God wants us to be full participants in our own lives.

Take a look now at your notion of divinity. Do you picture God in human form? As male or female? Or perhaps God takes an animal form, or the form of a flower or a mountain. Whatever image you choose, see the advantages and disadvantages of picturing God in this way. After a few minutes of imagining God, move in the opposite direction, by negating any image of God that arises in the mind's eye.

From Me to Meaning

I reject the false narratives of endless greed and competition. I live and work for the good of all beings, seeking to make the world a more caring place.

We can sometimes think, when times are hard, that we must have taken a wrong turn or done something bad to deserve our fate. But no one ever promised an easy or trouble-free life. The idea that we should be happy all of the time comes mostly from advertising copy. Mindfulness is not about just being happy; it goes much deeper than that. Mindfulness leads to a greater identification with the sufferings of human and nonhuman others. It leads to an increased sense of solidarity with all beings. That can sometimes lead to happiness, but it would be perverse to want neverending happiness in a world filled with so much suffering and injustice.

Today, bind yourself to the fate of all creatures. Resolve to feel for others and do what you can to alleviate suffering. Set aside the me, me, me ethic of consumer capitalism and seek rather to build a meaningful life for yourself through service. See there in the cave of the heart the trials of all human beings and plant and animal life as well. Hold the world there in your compassionate embrace.

Send Gratitude to All

I am ever mindful of the many good things and good people in the world. I give thanks for the ordinary lives all around me, for those who carry the load but do not get much credit. I honor those who make the world go around with their silent toil.

Remember that the good, honest, trustworthy people rarely make the news. So we can get the sense that unscrupulous and even criminal behavior is pervasive when in reality only a small subsection of people lie, cheat, and steal as a way of life. The majority of people are generally honest and trustworthy. In order to get along in life, we have to let down our defenses and trust others. We simply can't go it alone. We need many skills and viewpoints to get along in life. A homogenous society is neither possible nor desirable.

As you sit here in the silence, enkindle a sense of gratitude for the many lives that touch your own. Think of the faces that you see each day, whether or not you can remember the names that belong to each person. Send each individual feelings of gratefulness and kindness. Radiate these good feelings to each person you meet for the rest of the day. Firmly determine to avoid a grumbling, negative disposition for the rest of this day.

Progress in Thirty-Minute Blocks

I prioritize my commitments according to my system of values. I concentrate my attention on the task at hand, working at maximum efficiency.

We work to our full potential when we complete one task at a time. Sure, you can work on a document while watching TV and folding laundry, but all three of those activities will suffer from divided attention. It makes much more sense to put all of the various tasks into a sequence and tackle them one at a time. Preferably we would do the most difficult thing first, but sometimes we have to make little bargains with our wayward minds. It's kind of like dealing with a toddler: okay, you do this one thing for half an hour, and then you can have a snack. Amazing progress can be made using thirty-minute blocks.

Today, set aside all social media and Internet use. Sit here quietly in this place of meditation, and ask for all distraction to be removed. Ask for the wisdom to prioritize the various tasks in your life in the best way possible. Ask for the fortitude to accomplish what needs to be done without complaining. When you leave this place, find the one thing in your life that most needs to be done, and devote at least thirty minutes to this task.

The Many Forms of Meditation

I tear down the dividing wall between myself and the world. I become more available and more present in all that I do. I no longer need to be isolated from others, to cower away from the world.

Anything can become a form of meditation if you approach it with the right attitude. Walking down the street, mowing the grass, reading the morning paper, or talking to someone at work become mindful activities when we stop holding back and start fully engaging with the experience. I think we fear losing ourselves in such encounters. We think that our selfhood resides in the inner monologue. Something much bigger awaits us when we let go of our defenses and allow our consciousness to rollick around in the world. We become more expansive, more bold, more compassionate, more caring, and more beautiful.

As you sit here in this sacred space, you may feel the urge to hold back. This may be manifested as an anxious hesitancy or a dull, lackluster feeling. Summon deep breathing, and allow the breath to overcome the internal resistance. Ask your childlike self to just try a new way of doing things for a few minutes. Speak tenderly to your mind, reassuring the hesitant voice that you won't allow any harm to come to it.

Growing Pains

I am open and willing to receive the guidance that life has for me.
I open myself to the changes now coming into my life.
I give myself fully to the work of transformation.

It is not uncommon to have minor or major dissociative experiences in meditation. You may look at yourself in the mirror and not recognize the person you see there. This is because your sense of self has expanded to the point where you no longer identify so much with the physical body. It can be hard to enter back into your old identity when you have been working so hard to think on a cosmic level. To ease these feelings, you might try expressing yourself through music, writing, or painting. You may also sense some changes in your preferences: you might suddenly like a new kind of food or prefer totally different fashions. This is just part of the harmonization that happens when you attune yourself more fully with the inner guide.

You may feel yourself being inwardly drawn in new directions in life. Open the heart center to receive spiritual guidance. Your job is not to supply advice to yourself or to reason with yourself. All you have to do is hold the inner space open and avoid filling in the silence with words and images. You may picture an inner door or aperture opening to the outside or to a bright light within. Just resolve to hold this stance of openness and listening as long as possible. The shape of your new identity will emerge, without a doubt.

Today Is the Day

I have the power within myself to make needed changes in my life. I have had more than enough delay, more than enough excuse-making. Today is the day when I will take decisive action to improve my own circumstances.

Change only happens in our lives when we want it badly enough, when it is just too painful to endure another day of the same old thing. A revolution must happen deep within, a strong determination to embark on a new course of action, whether that might be looking for a new job, getting more exercise, or going back to school. The initial changes may prove difficult, but, with each action taken, the new path comes to seem easier and gradually becomes a new routine. But change never happens without that inner resolve, followed by decisive action.

You may have some life change that you would like to make today. Look deep within yourself and feel the vibration of assent flowing through your being. Feel yourself saying yes to all of the easy and difficult changes that you will make. Feel yourself saying yes to the renegotiation of duties and relationships. See yourself succeeding in your mind's eye, taking up a whole new way of life. Immediately take action to put your life change into motion.

Untested Assumptions

I give myself the permission to question the stories that I tell myself. I give myself the ability to deviate from the self-limiting scripts that hold me in place.

Most of us live under many false premises that we rarely question. We say to ourselves, so-and-so will not love me if I do not do X for him or her. Or I will lose my job if I do not work eighty-hour weeks. Or if I do not give X amount to charity, I must be a bad person. We can find more freedom by acting in our own best interests and letting the chips fall where they may. The people in our lives may not be as unreasonable as we think, and we may not have to typecast ourselves so strictly into a predictable role. We have to learn to separate our versions of reality from reality itself—the stories that we tell ourselves from the way things are.

What is a story that you tell yourself to keep from having to take some beneficial risk in your life? Take a long hard look at that story right now. Could you be exaggerating it in some way? Could you be extrapolating what happened on one occasion into a general law of the universe? Allow yourself to deviate from the mental constructs that confine you. Picture what it would be like to break the rules that you have set for yourself.

Over the Long Haul

I find calm in the midst of a busy day in the quiet chamber of my heart. I find peace and contentment within, and I share my blessings with everyone I meet.

Now that you have found mindfulness and meditation, you know how to light a candle for yourself in a dark place. The trick is to remember that you already know how to calm yourself, that you can take a silent retreat anytime you need one. The temptation will be strong to forget what you have learned and go back to a frantic way of life. Commit to the life of mindfulness not just for a few days or a year, but for the rest of your time on earth. The practice may feel dull and dry from time to time, but it will greatly increase your sense of well-being over the long term.

As you sit here in this quiet place, give yourself the luxury of this time apart. Set your sights on more than just survival and accumulation of material goods. Allow yourself to be completely well and completely balanced as you synchronize your mind with your environment. The mind is in tune with the breath. The breath is in touch with the vital air. The mind and the surroundings become one.

Setting Aside Cynicism

*I may not see an immediate way out of my problems, but I remain
open to the inner guide. I know that, when I sincerely and patiently ask,
I will receive the wisdom that I seek.*

We all get a payoff of sorts by remaining cynical, by believing that we are stuck in life, and by thinking that change is impossible, on a personal and societal level. If we don't believe that change is possible, we get to sit on our cans and do nothing. Once we believe in the possibility of change, suddenly we have a job to do. So our task as practitioners of creative spirituality is twofold: first, continuing to stoke belief in personal and world transformation, and, second, to act in concordance with our deepest beliefs. When these two aspects work together, we can change our own lives and the societies in which we live.

Today, let go of the cynical attitudes that hold you back. Disavow and detach from that part of your personality that must always scoff at anything positive, that must always poke holes in any transformative project or theory. Move into that part of your own mind that hopes against all odds and believes in the possibility of human goodness. Let this aspect of your personality go free for a few minutes, and resolve to loosen it even further as you go throughout this day.

Spreading the Light

*I understand the cosmic law that what I send into the universe
returns to me. I make myself a vessel for peace and understanding
in order to make the world a better place.*

I occasionally hear from readers who are overjoyed at the change that they see in their lives from the simple practice of mindfulness and silent listening. Most people come looking for nothing more than a little bit of stress relief, but they find more than they ever wanted. They find transformed relationships, inner joy, and solutions to problems. The insurmountable obstacles fade before the steady, daily practice of meditation. Meanwhile, there is nothing complex about the practice, nothing that can't be explained in a few minutes. But the rewards are real and long-lasting.

Feel a sense of gratitude for all that you have learned about yourself and about life through your practice of meditation. Hold in your heart center those dear to you and those you do not know. Feel compassion for the people in your life and those you have never met. Think of a few small ways that you can spread the light of mindfulness in unobtrusive ways.

Facing That Big, Huge Problem

As I open my mind and heart, new connections begin to form.
A path opens to me that was unknown before. I move beyond all obstacles
and obtain the blessings of life.

All of us are troubled at times by problems that linger, year after year. These situations have been placed in our lives to get us to expand our self-definitions beyond the comfortable confines of the lives we have known so far. We overcome these persistent problems by becoming bigger people, by doing and being more than we ever thought possible. We expand our reach and our capabilities until what had previously seemed like an insurmountable obstacle now seems manageable. The nagging problem comes to be less of a millstone and more of a springboard, giving impetus to ever more expansion in self-discovery.

Bring to mind now the biggest problem in your life, together with any emotions and sensations that go along with that. You may feel a tightening in the chest or feelings of panic. Through lengthening the breath and inner observation, bring your anxiety down to a manageable level. Continue in the practice until you feel completely calm. Then ask for three small things you can do to make that big problem more manageable. When you leave the sacred space, take action.

Second Sight

I listen to the whispers of eternity in the midst of time.
I strain my ears to listen to the subtle voice. I pull aside the veil between
the divine and human worlds.

Just beyond the reach of ordinary consciousness lies a completely different way of perceiving the world. In this mode of being, a thing is not just a thing but a vibrant presence, a glowing radiance. In order to access this way of seeing, we only need to be open to it. In this way of being, we set aside our personal agendas and simply attend to the things as they present themselves. When the inner dialogue arises, we set it aside. And, with good timing and a good deal of perseverance, a moment dawns in which we are completely in tune with our surroundings.

Today, try meditating with your eyes open, preferably somewhere in nature where you will not be disturbed. Find a focal point, like the bark of a tree or a flower, and focus your attention completely on that object. You must be very strict with yourself and allow no distraction. Allow the object of your attention to fill your consciousness, so that nothing remains except the encounter. Hold this intensity for as long as possible. If it becomes too difficult, you can start a little dialogue saying, "I want to see you as you truly are."

An Audience of None

I persevere in good times and bad times, when things go my way and when things do not. I push past my limits over and over again, and, in this way, I conquer every obstacle.

Whether we think life is fair or unfair, there is not much to do but keep on going. The people in my life, for example, are not just going to drop everything and wait until I get into the right mood to do my work. These people—my family, my coworkers, my clients, my students—all depend on me, and I have a duty to respond to them. We all have to do our duty, however falteringly or imperfectly, as this responsibility makes the human world livable. Duty is not always or even usually exciting, but its constancy keeps the world from spiraling out of control. When we fulfill our duty, we may not receive a lot of fanfare and recognition, but we earn the satisfaction of having done what is right.

For every hero story, there are a thousand who did equally important jobs but received no praise. Today, as you sit here in the quiet, let go of the need for rewards and recognition. Let go of the need to be noticed for doing your job or taking care of your family. Surrender this aspect of the self that wants to be seen doing what is right. Surrender the aspect of the self that wants credit for work done. Content yourself with doing your work anonymously, with no audience, not even the audience of one.

Born for Bliss

My heart breaks free from the shackles of convention. I will not be confined by the opinions and beliefs of others. I make my way confidently and boldly into the divine life allotted for me before the world began.

Even after months or years of meditation, you may still find yourself caring an awful lot about what other people think of you. You may hold back in your practice and in the way that you live your life for fear that someone will call you crazy, overzealous, or naive. But the world desperately needs the good kind of crazy. The world needs people who are crazy-centered, crazy-loving, and crazy-kind. If someone laughs at you, fine, let them laugh! At least you will have lived by your own muses, by your own lights. And your own heart will not be dulled by that calculating instinct that must second-guess every action.

Close your eyes and enter into deep breathing as usual. Observe the thoughts and emotions as they arise. When you catch yourself getting distracted, say, "I was born for this, I was born for bliss. I was born for this moment, I was born for bliss." You can stop repeating the phrase for a while, and then go back to it as soon as distraction arises again.

Lowering the Alert Level

I make time, my friend, by diligently using each day that is given to me.
I learn self-discipline, so that I become faithful in big things
and small things. I can trust myself with my own affairs.

Perhaps you have some failures in your past that have led you to doubt yourself. Maybe you have been divorced or lost a job or let someone down. It can be hard to recover trust in yourself, especially if you continually recite a list of past failures. This trust comes back little by little, after many faltering steps and many small victories. Gradually we learn to stop blaming ourselves, and we allow ourselves to think that maybe, just maybe, things are going to be okay.

You may find yourself conditioned to anticipate some calamity just around the corner. Especially when things are going well, you may ask yourself, "Okay, when is the other shoe going to drop?" If you have this tendency, take a look at it in your mind's eye. Call it into question now. What supports and sustains this guardedness, this alertness to risk? Could it perhaps be the case that you have entered into a new phase of your life, where what was once a defining issue for you can now recede?

Ends and Beginnings

I realize that, however good my analytic skills, I will have to live into an uncertain future. I do not put my trust in the prevailing power structures, but I take refuge within the calm center of my being.

It can be so easy to get discouraged with all of the bad news out there. Sometimes it feels as though the world is falling apart. But it must have felt that way to the ancient Romans as well, and the Greeks before that, and the Mycenaeans before that. Civilizations rise and fall: they are just as impermanent as anything else in existence. Why should our time be any different? The corruption that we see, the degradation of the environment, and the warped priorities are all signs of decline. But every end contains a beginning, a chance to start over.

The future, by definition, is uncertain. You may catch yourself today trying to guess what will happen in politics or in technology. Let go of this future-watching for the time being. Concentrate on the here and now, on this inner space that arises before the mind. Take shelter here, knowing that, whatever happens, you will still be able to retreat within and concentrate on the breath.

Celebrating Your Wholeness

I exercise my intelligence, my compassion, my willing, and my loving,
knowing that the best choices come from the whole person.
I allow all parts of nature to speak equally,
listening to the best voices that I have within me.

Most of us have learned to hate some part of ourselves through the messages that we receive from the culture. Speaking in generalities, men are generally taught to hide their emotions and keep them buried, while women are taught to despise their bodies in various ways. All of us have forms of shame, around creative expression, around the use of money, or around sexuality. We come to meditation and mindfulness with all of these deep-seated cultural biases and expectations. Our practice must bring these things to light, expose the various unfair standards under which we live, and then suggest more liberative ways of living that free the hidden parts of ourselves.

Is there a part of yourself that is longing to be brought into the open? What is it? Picture yourself now, expressing the hidden part of you that wants to be free. Can you find a supportive person or a supportive environment that might help you to expose this vulnerable part of yourself? Imagine what it would be like to no longer have to suppress that part of your personality.

Making the Leap

I do not wait for complete certainty before making a choice: I gather a modicum of information and then make the leap into the next stage of my life. I realize the benefits of decisive action in the present.

Spending a lot of time deliberating about a given decision doesn't necessarily equate to reaching a better outcome. Debating the pros and cons and doing empirical research can be important, but there are also costs associated with delaying action. Sometimes we just have to make our best guess and move ahead. Those around us will appreciate a certain amount of decisiveness, and there will be time later to correct any errors and make course corrections. All of us must deal with moving targets and the swift passage of time.

As you sit here in the silence, ask for the removal of obstacles in all areas of your life. Bring wholeness and completeness into your body and your mind. Ask for blessings on your labor and your projects. See your emotions coming into a balanced and harmonious state. See your network of friends and contacts expanding. See yourself growing in terms of your connection to the life of the spirit. Will that everyone in your life have these same aspects of well-being. As soon as you leave the meditation space, go straightaway to work to make these things a reality.

Don't Panic, Plan!

I turn aside from anxiety and look for ways to work peacefully.
I break each task down into its component parts and take things
one step at a time. I become skilled at working under pressure,
and I feel calm in the midst of activity.

Our old reactive circuits tend to activate when we have a big deadline looming on the horizon. We often have to depend upon other people to do their parts of a project before the final product can be assembled. It will do no good to kvetch about peers missing deadlines: we have to do what we can to control what we can control and forget the rest. Getting even a small start does much to ease the mind. It also helps to allow yourself a rough draft, a practice version. Something as simple as jotting down a few ideas on a sheet of scratch paper can help you find calm.

You may have one or two projects on your mind right now that are making you rigid and tense. You may want to bite your nails or scream or burst a blood vessel. Speak calmly to yourself. Slow down the breath. Reverse the stress response. Sit here in the quiet, knowing that the very moment you return to your work a plan will emerge for how you can tackle your problems. A plan will present itself with steps that you can take to reduce your burden.

Keys of Greatness

I may be afraid, but I do not let my fear hold me back. I keep moving forward in the unfolding of my divine destiny.

We all hold the keys to Self-realization in our own hands, but we balk at our own greatness. We fear stepping into the unknown. We fear greater expression of the divine principle in our lives. We have immense creativity and many wonderful skills, but we hold ourselves back. We fear the exposure that comes with living up to our full potential. It is more comfortable for most of us to be a wallflower than to be the star of the show. It is more comfortable not to try than it is to face rejection. But we were born for full participation in this beautiful world; we just have to pluck up our courage and act.

Come with me to a place where you have everything that you need in order to manifest your full potential. At your fingertips are the materials that you need to build the creation of your dreams. At your fingertips are the contacts that you need to find assistance along the way. Whispering into your ear are the teachers and muses who will lead the way. Flowing into your heart is the willingness and the eagerness to be underway. Your whole being, mind, body, and spirit, pulses with vibrant life, ready to undertake the mission of a lifetime.

At the End of the Rope

*When I am presented with great pain and loss,
I embrace the way that remains open to me. I know that I will find a way
when all other options have been exhausted.*

We begin to succeed in life when failure is not an option. I do not intend this as some sort of macho statement: sometimes we just have to reach our wit's end before change becomes possible. We have to be fed up with the old reality before the new one can emerge. That very painful breaking point becomes the impetus to move in a new direction. Just like we yank our hands away from a hot fire, we naturally turn away from the pain of a situation that isn't working. At that moment, the new way presents itself, and the solution becomes clear.

Have you ever hit rock bottom before? Are you in that place right now? There is a new way for you, one that does not involve harming yourself or others. You can be a perfectly sane and balanced person while also doing the work that your heart desires. You can have food, shelter, and clothing while also doing the work that your heart desires. You can have strong, light-hearted relationships while also doing the work that your heart desires. All of this is possible and more: you just have to reach out and grab hold of it.

Real-Life Heroes

I understand that all of my heroes and idols are ordinary people, just like myself. I, too, have exceptional abilities that are only waiting for the opportunity to be expressed.

When I was a kid, sometime in the 1980s, I met the actor Lou Ferrigno, who played the character of the Incredible Hulk on television, which was one of my favorite shows at the time. It was a weird encounter for me, because, there he was, just a normal guy. To be sure, he was still pretty muscular, but he wasn't green, and he was just wearing regular clothes. We can sometimes make our heroes into superhuman beings, but they are all normal people just like ourselves. And because this is true, it means that we, too, are capable of more than we think.

You may be thinking now of someone whom you idolized as a kid or someone whom you still idolize. Those same good qualities that you admire in your hero already reside within yourself. See yourself tending and nurturing these qualities. Feel these qualities getting stronger inside your heart even now. Picture yourself growing into full maturity, so that your life comes closer and closer to the cherished ideal.

Loving and Losing

I love those who remain in my life and those who have departed. I hold a space of goodwill in my heart for all those whose lives have touched my own.

People come and go from our lives. Sometimes this separation happens naturally through the course of events. Sometimes we actively push people away. Sometimes we are the ones doing the pushing, and sometimes we are the ones pushed. All relationships must necessarily change. We can still love those who have passed out of our lives completely. We can still love them, even if we are no longer speaking. We can have the peace of knowing that the good and bad times in the past all really happened, and we can make way for the new experiences now arriving.

Make a wide, loving space in your heart. See past and present folded into one present reality. All of the people whom you love are there, whether they are living or dead, nearby or far away. See this great crowd in your heart center, feasting and dancing. You are those whom you love, and they are you. Each one is an aspect of yourself, and they also reflect some aspect of you. See these many faces as aspects of the divine nature as it manifests itself in love.

The Web of Life

Sometimes life brings us crushing pain and loss. In times like these,
we hold to each other and draw strength from community.

A friend of mine in college committed suicide freshman year, and the brutal fact of this occurrence was like a bomb going off in my set of friends. It was simply inexplicable: she was so young, bright, and well-liked. We all came together in the aftermath, even though we would eventually drift apart. This experience taught me that sometimes there is no reason, no explanation for why bad things happen. Sometimes moralizing and religiosity is just no use. Sometimes we just have to sit there in the pain and give each other what little comfort we can.

Picture all of the relationships in your life as one huge web, each relationship as one strand within that web. Anything that touches one life within that web touches all parts of the web, and the vibrations are felt, near and far. It follows, then, that whatever you bring into your heart today will also be passed along to everyone who belongs to the web. Note also that there are no logical stopping points, no such thing as a purely local event. Bring into your heart now joy, peace, and tranquility, knowing that you do this for all of those who share the earth with you.

No Shortfalls

I let go of the false belief that there is no abundance in store for me.
I believe in the possibility of a full, rich, and rewarding life, and my actions
and dispositions flow from this basic understanding.

There is no shortage of good ideas, only a shortage of people to bring them to full fruition. Maybe this is what Jesus meant when he said that the harvest is plentiful, but the laborers are few (Matthew 9:37). Almost everyone on earth has several good ideas, some of them potentially world changing. But, in order for them to work, they have to make their way into a usable form. As creative spiritual practitioners, we are people of good thoughts and intentions, yes, but we are also people of action. We are willing to not just espouse high-minded principles but also to bring them into our daily lives.

Have you ever had a good idea that fell flat? Maybe you tried really hard, but still nothing came of that idea. Open up your heart now to your sense of disappointment. Open yourself to the possibility of going back to that project that died on the vine. Open yourself to the possibility of new insights coming to you now that will help that idea once again see the light of day. Know that someone in your life may already have the resources you need to get back on the right track.

On Recovery

Although things may have fallen apart in one area of my life, I maintain the possibility of rebuilding. As I do what I can to bring restoration, I find that, ever so gradually, the balance tips in the favor of wellness and wholeness.

When we face setbacks in life, in terms of health, wealth, or relationships, it is very important to think not about what we can no longer do but about what we can still do. We have to take charge in the areas where we have some capacity. Making progress in one small area of life then makes it easier to improve other areas. Recovery from some major setback will take time, but the pace will be faster if we avoid doom-and-gloom, fatalistic thinking. We just have to find one fragment of our lives that is still relatively intact and then build from there. In order to think big, we must first learn, once again, how to think small.

Right now you might not be in a place to think about attaining enlightenment (whatever that word means for you). Think instead about what brings you joy today, what makes you want to live today. Maybe nothing at all comes to mind, and that is perfectly fine. Sit here in openness to the idea that life is worth living, that there is some reason that you are still alive. You don't even need to think positively; just turn away the negative thoughts when they come.

Thank Your Survival Instincts

I have come so far down this road, and I have learned to make my way through all difficulties. Trusting in my deepest self, I move forward confidently.

Remember that many times in your life already you have encountered situations that felt like the end of the world. You have been sure many times in the past that you would no longer be able to earn a living, that no one would love you, or that your body would no longer function. Each time you found a creative solution, you found a way to keep on going; you found a way to keep your head above water. As a simple extrapolation from past experience, know that whatever you face today, you can and will survive. You will go beyond mere survival to thriving in this lifetime. The knowledge of how to overcome any obstacles in your path already lies within you, otherwise you would not be sitting here today.

Give thanks now for having come so far in life. Give thanks for the times that you were sure your life was over, for the times you were saved just in time. Give thanks for the skills and abilities that you have gained over the years and for the people who have helped you along the way. Know, deep inside yourself, that you have what you need to get through the difficult times that may arise. Let go of fear and live in peace.

The Reality of Change

I know that everything in my life changes.
I bend to the reality of change and become more flexible and adaptable.
I accept pain as proof that I am still alive.

There is always a little bit of pain associated with change: the pain of letting go of the familiar routine and trying something new. There is the pain of perhaps having to let go of something held dear and the fear that perhaps the new reality will be worse than the old one. This pain of having to change is the background to all of life, as we are always moving from one state and into another. In itself, this pain is nothing bad. It is our response to this background condition that determines whether we make progress or regress. On some level, we must embrace pain as the price of admission: we have to accept the reality of change and move along with it.

Look now at the change occurring in your own life. You may see yourself resisting change, bargaining with it, denying change, but there it is. Move toward accepting change and welcoming it. Observe any pain associated with change, and welcome pain as well, as it reminds you that you are still alive.

You Said Yes

I know that many wonderful adventures await me in life,
and I avoid getting mired in past habits. I say yes to the good things now
coming to me, and I become more awake and alive.

Every good thing in your life came to you because you were open to it in some way. You said yes to something or someone. You showed up at the interview. You went on the date. You opened the book. And now, in your life at this very moment, new opportunities wait for you. These opportunities are not rare or inaccessible: they are all around you, just waiting to be discovered. Your life ten years from now will depend upon the choices that you make today, on your ability to say yes to the many opportunities in your life. If you accept even a few of them, you can change everything, and for the better.

As you sit here in the darkness, work on overturning the old habits of mind. Thoughts will come to you that you have seen a hundred or a thousand times before. They may take on different guises, but recognize them as the same old mental noise in a different package. Look for something arising in your mind that you have never seen before. See a glimmer of the new, a glimmer of something so astounding and surprising that it takes your breath away. If it does not come, refuse to budge an inch, and stick to interior quiet.

Orderly States

I take the time to order my space and order my mind. When the disturbing thoughts arise, I take shelter in the calm center of my being.

When feeling stuck on a project, get up and take a walk. Then spend fifteen to twenty minutes cleaning the workspace: put excess papers in the recycling, put books back on the shelf, and take care of minor administrative details. Then go back to work. You will find that the mind only needs a short break to reset itself. The decluttered workspace also leads to a calmer mind, and the work will proceed smoothly after taking a short but productive break. Progress leads to progress.

You may have in your head now a kind of cramped, fatigued feeling, like you simply cannot concentrate a second longer. Simply observe this feeling, including any words or phrases that arise. You may also notice physical sensations, like the beginnings of a tension headache or a nervous stomach. Retreat, in your mind's eye, to the back of the body, toward the spinal column, and down the body, toward the heart center. Establish yourself here, in the calm center, where no disturbing thoughts can go.

Work and Comfort

I surround myself with small luxuries that make my work pleasant and light.
I acknowledge my body as the seat of my genius,
as the source of joys and imaginings.

A good workspace must provide not only functionality but also creature comforts: a good chair, a nice lamp, some hot tea or coffee. The body is not just a hat rack for the head; it has needs and priorities of its own. If it is kept happy, it will not protest at long hours of work. A quick break for yoga, a snack here and there, a few minutes of music—all of these offerings to the restless body will make it receptive. The ideas, too, will improve, as embodiment makes a positive contribution to the making of meaning.

Observe now any harsh attitudes that you take toward your body. Take a few minutes to do an internal scan of your entire body, moving from the tip of your toes to the crown of your head. Pause along the way at any parts of your body that you do not like or that cause you pain. Send love and healing toward those parts of yourself that you have a hard time accepting. Make friends with your body as your companion in life.

Lessons along the Way

*I learn from my work each day, growing in my skills and understanding.
I do not shrink from the challenges or the lessons of this day,
but I grow into greater maturity and responsibility.*

Before making it to my career goal as a writer and professor, I had jobs as a clerk in a drug store, as a data entry person, as a prep cook, as a waiter, among many other such jobs. Not one of these positions was exactly hell on earth for me: every one of them had redeeming features. Every one gave me some sort of knowledge about the world that I was lacking before. Every one helped me to mature a little bit (I am still not all the way there). If you are in a position that you don't love, take heart: this is not the last job you will ever have. Even if it is the last job you will ever have, look for those bright spots, those enjoyable aspects of your day that make it worthwhile.

You may be hating your job today or loving your job today. Even if you are unemployed, you still have work to do today. Be thankful for the ability to be productive, for the ability to be involved in something useful, even if it is not lucrative or glamorous. Resolve today to be kind to each person you meet, to be gracious under pressure, and to make your workplace better in some small way. Look upon each action as a chance to enkindle the divine spark.

Learning to Smile Again

I look for opportunities for play, for fun, for silliness.
I exercise my creativity and my imagination. I look for my inner happiness.

Years of worry drag our faces down into a perpetual frown, so that it requires a little bit of work to smile. We associate worry and frustration with being a full-grown adult, but it doesn't have to be that way, at least not all the time. We can be lighthearted and joyful without losing sight of our goals or neglecting our responsibilities. We can be happy and prudent at the same time, as awkward as that juxtaposition seems. Mindfulness gives us that little nudge, that reminder to look for the smile, from the inside out.

As you are sitting here in meditation, smile with your eyes closed. Smooth the furrows in your brow, and smile with your eyes as well. Make the smile a little broader, as though you had just seen someone you had been missing for many years. You may notice a brighter emotional state, and you may also feel a little ridiculous. See if you can take that smile with you as you leave this place, and try to be a little more lighthearted for the rest of this day.

Super and Natural

*I accept that there are aspects of reality that exceed my grasp,
and I make way for the unexpected to occur in my life.*

What we call the supernatural is really a subdivision of the natural world: namely, that which we do not yet understand. We can also call supernatural cures the enhanced placebo effect, which refers to the power of the mind not to override matter but to make previously unnoticed connections between domains that had been separate. The common sense approach of one century is the superstition of the next century, or it may also be that what is considered superstition today becomes the common sense of tomorrow. The bottom line is that we do not fully appreciate our own capabilities, and more is possible in the universe than we can ever imagine.

Think for a few minutes about the notion that what you believe to be impossible may actually be possible. Sit here in openness to what you do not understand, and invite the unexpected into your life. Prepare yourself for something genuinely new and surprising, for the overturning of tired categories of understanding. Make way for novel connections and interactions.

Two Gardeners

I give thanks to this earth, which feeds me and shelters me.
I am willing to do my part to bring peace and harmony to all beings.

Let's suppose a gardener were to put some seeds in the ground and then just leave them there, without weeding and watering them. Then his neighbor also plants some seeds, but spends time each day carefully tending them. Which gardener will get the best results? So it is with our spiritual lives: we have to work at becoming better people every day, inside and out. It will be difficult, but it will yield better results than half-measures.

Touch the ground now in front of your seat. Say thanks to Mother Earth for giving you this time of contemplation. Allow Her to strengthen you, and allow Her to dispel all of your demons. Surrender to Her, and allow Her to show you the realm of bliss that She has been waiting to reveal to you. Entrust your life to Her, and give over all of your affairs into Her care. She will not fail to make you free.

Physical Challenge

*I recognize that my physical well-being is an intrinsic
part of having mental health. I live into greater activity,
pushing myself in new directions and making myself strong.*

Physical exercise is not really optional for those of us who want to lead productive and meaningful lives. To be sure, we can have a few sedentary years, but they will catch up to us sooner or later. Better to go ahead and take charge of the situation by going to the yoga studio or gym, by walking, running, or swimming. At least once a year, we should all stretch our capacities by doing something we did not believe we could do, like climbing a mountain or learning a new sport. Any physical limitations need not be obstacles. We can work around them to improve quality of life.

Do you have in mind, right now, something that you believe you physically cannot do? Take a long, hard look at that belief. Is it a self-created illusion, or is it rooted in reality? Can you, with minor modifications, make a more active life for yourself? Can you step up your game just a little? Is there some crazy goal you could pursue to make life more enjoyable? Inquire and then do.

Finely Aged

I refuse to throw away my life with regret and fantasy.
I come to terms with my own stage in life, and I make my stand here.
I can find meaning and joy at any age, no matter my circumstances.

The fixation on youthfulness is one of the many pathologies of consumer culture. Overvaluing youth devalues the rest of life, making middle age and the senior years—which is to say, the majority of time that most of us have on earth—into throwaway afterthoughts. Think about finely aged wines and Stradivarius violins: some things get better with age. We must retrain ourselves and our culture to value every person in every phase of life and to stop chasing after the dream of perpetual youth.

Search your mind for idealized images of youthfulness. It may be difficult or painful, but dismiss these images one by one. Let go of the need to hold on to the past, to be that person that you once were. Realize that all of these images are illusory, fantasy versions only loosely based on reality. Live more deeply into the time that you have now. Reconcile yourself to this time, this body, this present.

Heading Off Crisis

I find peace in life through diligence and efficiency. I address problems as soon as I notice them, rather than waiting for them to become worse.

As we mature and develop, we learn the value of spotting problems before they become problems, to act before the crisis arises, to make life easier through anticipation. This mature way of thinking and acting saves both time and money, not to mention a lot of stress and anxiety. We also come to know our own limits, to ask for expert guidance and help when necessary. The haphazard approach of youthfulness gives way to foresight and planning. Maybe that sounds boring, but it also induces calm.

As you are sitting here in the darkness, you may be troubled by thoughts of what might go wrong with your home, with your career, or with your relationships. Acknowledge these thoughts, but do not engage with them. Do not engage in dark visions of panic or anxiety. Simply take note and move on. When you have finished meditating, make a list of things that you can do to address the troublesome parts of your life.

Less Is More

I turn aside from the desire for possessions and entertainments.
I hold to simplicity, within and without, and I find contentment.

Strive to speak less and listen more, to want less and be more. Hold to simplicity, and gain everything. The desire for ever more possessions leads only to entrapment, as the person becomes the servant of wealth. Consider as necessary a table, a cup, a bowl, and a chair. Consider as unnecessary marble staircases and gilt fireplaces. The person who is centered within lacks for nothing, while the person who has no calm center can never be satisfied. We find this law at work everywhere.

As you shut your eyes to meditate, come into close contact with your own interior state. Sense the outlines of your own body, the feeling of your chest rising and falling with the breath. Sense the spaciousness of this vessel, its dark contours. Let this space be enough for you. Strive to be happy to remain here in your own body, to want nothing more than what you already have. Entertain no flights of fancy, no thoughts of escape. Be at home here, and you will be at home everywhere.

Setting Knowledge Aside

I set aside my knowledge about the world,
and I encounter people and things directly, without any intermediary.
I live into a different way of knowing that is based on silent listening.

I am a person with an inordinate fondness for books and learning, but that can also be a liability in many ways. There are things that cannot be known by reading books, even the most esoteric or profound texts. In order to really know, we have to set aside everything that we think we know. We have to disallow a single letter to remain and gaze onto nature without interpreting it. It can be very hard to set aside mental frameworks, to avoid imposing our categories onto reality. But this is the necessary task for the practice of meditation and mindfulness. This act of setting knowledge aside makes possible our return to the source.

As you close your eyes, your mind will rush to your rescue, trying to be helpful. It will provide snatches of background music, suggestions for what to do later today, recipes to make for dinner, and the name of that one weird kid in elementary school. You cannot actually stop the mind from doing this. Just allow the flow to come and go without engaging. Pay attention to the occasional silences, and see if you can make them expand.

One-Track Mind

I focus on the present moment while keeping the bigger picture in mind.
I squirrel away time to make my vision a reality.

A one-track mind is not such a bad thing to be born with, so long as you can direct the mind toward something worthwhile. Generally, those things worth achieving are long-range goals that do not provide instant satisfaction. Months or years of work may be necessary to see these worthwhile goals come to fruition. But the task itself provides enough fodder for the mind, to keep it engaged in useful problem-solving. This focus on the task, on the process, becomes indispensable for achieving higher-level goals.

Ask yourself today why you are living, in a long-term sense. What could you do if you had a few years or a few decades? See if a vision arises for you of something difficult but inspiring, something that you could do with enough dedication and practice. After leaving this place, set aside a little bit of time for that long-range goal, for that something beautiful you want to do with your life.

Idea and Execution

I strive to shorten the gap between idea and execution,
trusting in my insight and ability. I perfect my craft while on the move,
changing my approach in response to conditions.

To get things done, we have to reduce the lag time between idea and execution. No plan ever arrives fully formed and error-free: the fixes happen in the creation of the thing. This is true whether we are talking about building a house, writing a book, or hiring a team. We should not be fooled into thinking that we are primarily cerebral creatures. Even in highly intellectual careers we still learn by doing. Meditation and mindfulness help us to cut directly to the chase, to remove the layers of obfuscation that prevent our plans from taking shape in the world.

Are you able to get beyond the planning stages and into execution? Think of one stalled plan in your life right now. What is preventing you from taking action? Try to understand the blockages in the way. Hold the problem there in your mind without a lot of monologue. See the most skillful way to intervene, so that the blockage is removed. Another way to approach this is to find the very simplest part of the problem, the thing done most easily. Go and do that.

Mindfulness As a Practical Skill

I recognize the management of my interior states as one of the most important skills in life. As I come to understand myself, I remove the obstacles to the achievement of any task in the world.

As creative spiritual practitioners we often get teased for being flighty and impractical. But I would be willing to bet on mindfulness and meditation as being highly effective life skills that can benefit anyone. These practices help us to get more satisfaction out of our working lives, and they help us to be more efficient and generate new insights. Through these practices we come to feel less like cogs in the machine and more like the whole people that we are. We are able to be more available to others without feeling drained all of the time. Self-observation translates into better outcomes on many levels.

You may feel helpless over your inner states right now. Know that you do not have to actively control them. Rather, shift your mind into the stance of observation. Look at the turbulent thoughts and emotions as they come into the inner space. Just be the observer, and the quality or tone of these thoughts and emotions will change. They will not go away, but they will become calmer and more beneficial. Just keep observing, and do not let them lead you around by the nose.

Individual Lessons

*I keep my practice simple but steady. I know that I can
consult the oracle of the heart for any question that I might have.
I espouse silence as my teacher, staying here in expectation.*

The practice of mindfulness does not require branded accessories or expensive seminars. The most valuable lessons that you learn will come when you are able to set aside some time and work on your own practice. Meditation teaches lessons specific to you as an individual, tailored to this exact time in your life. You can find answers to the questions that are important to you that may not be addressed in mass market guidance. Simply speak your question silently before you sit, and then proceed with the practice. The answer may not come right away, but it will come.

Only ask questions of the inner guide that warrant such a method of seeking. Ask the big life questions, the ones requiring discernment of values. Simply pose the question now into the inner space. Set a timer for a predetermined period, say ten, twenty, or sixty minutes. You may receive some guidance. If you do not, try repeating the process or doing some spiritual journaling.

Mindfulness and Messiness

I do not wait for the perfect moment to come.
I do not wait for free time to magically appear.
I make my practice a priority and do not wait for permission to begin.

Mindfulness need not wait for ideal conditions. You don't need to get your life together so that you can start meditating. You don't need a budget or an expense account. You don't need permission from your boss or your spouse or your mom. You just need the willingness to find greater clarity in life and a few minutes or hours set aside for this purpose. If you feel like your life is a mess, great! You have plenty of materials with which to work. Just notice things: your thoughts and emotions, flowers and children and birds.

Congratulations on having set this time apart for the practice! Take a break now from to-do lists, spreadsheets, and memos. Retreat into the vast chamber of the spinal column, which may be visualized as a tower, cathedral, or temple. Light the lamp of the heart, and allow the vital breath to stoke the flame. Sit here in observation, here where nothing can hurt you. Become very strong and fierce, and return to the world only when ready.

The Way to Freedom

*I remain awake to the fact that situations will come along
that seek to disturb my calm. I refuse to rise to the bait,
and I keep my heart and mind calm and clear.*

If we want to free ourselves, we have to let go of all feelings of entitlement. We have to renounce the idea that we have a right to be angry or sad or disgruntled in response to situations that are usually pretty trivial. Entitled emotions are basically self-created and useless, false friends that do not serve us in life. We have to deal with what is real and no longer engage in the dramas of life. To be sure, we will still be existing normally in the world, but we know to expect that those false friends, the negative emotions, will try to draw our attention away from that which is important. We become more vigilant and watchful.

You probably have some unwritten rules of your psyche that prevent you from having peace in life. Such a rule takes the form of an if-then formula: if someone does X to me, then I have to respond by doing Y. As you look at your mental landscape, can you see traces of such a reactive approach? Keep in mind that your reactions may be directed outward, through retaliatory behavior, subtle or unsubtle, or directed inward, through self-harming behavior, subtle or unsubtle. See if you can discover some of these hidden rules, and, by eliminating or revising them, find freedom.

What Matters and What Does Not

I take the time to discriminate between what I truly value and what I do not. I make all of my actions and affections align with my highest beliefs, and, in this way, I find freedom.

The most important thing: to be clear about what matters and what does not matter. The second most important thing: to act in accordance with what does and does not matter. If we do not adequately attend to these questions, we will fall prey to the false beliefs readily available in society. If we don't decide for ourselves, someone else will decide for us. Mindfulness just asks us to be intentional about what we think, feel, believe, and do, to live contemplatively rather than reactively.

See if you can state what is most important to you in a few words. Spend some time reflecting on these highest priorities. Dig a little deeper: are they really your highest objectives? Or do you have some unstated goals that you don't like admitting to yourself? Hold in your mind for a few minutes your highest objective in life, excluding all else. You will know you are coming close to your destiny when the thought of your highest ideal fills you with joy.

Reality Check

I find patience and calm within my own heart. If I find patience and calm in one situation, I can find patience and calm in any situation.

Before getting upset, ask yourself these two questions: did someone die? Is my personal safety in jeopardy? If the answer to either of these questions is yes, then, by all means, get upset and ask someone for help. But if the answer is no, slow down, breathe deeply, and take no drastic measures. Work through the situation deliberately, staying centered in the present moment. Think of the most constructive and beneficial response, both for yourself and others. Then act.

Cultivate a feeling now of patience, of calm abiding. Make your posture more upright, breathe deeply, and act as though you had all the time in the world. Picture yourself holding this posture for days and years and aeons. Picture yourself as the emblem of eternity, as a symbol of great strength and resolve in uncertain times. Become the peace and strength that you want to bring into your life.

Finishing Projects

I divest myself of my past tendency to walk away from my projects and plans. I develop the resolve to see all things through to completion.

Completing our duties, reducing our desires, keeping our commitments: these are all ways to free ourselves from worldly attachments. When we leave things undone, they don't go away. They just come back again later, and often appear in an exacerbated form. Anything we can do to simplify life will be beneficial, anything we can do to reduce indebtedness helps us, and anything we can do to solve a problem in a lasting way is in our best interest. We have to act like people who don't have long to live, as though a sense of urgency compels us to settle our affairs and get things squared away. That is the kind of attitude that leads to liberation.

Do you have a habit of leaving things undone? Think of three things in your life in need of completion. Then see yourself as already having the strength and wherewithal to complete them. See yourself smoothly moving through the steps necessary. As soon as you leave the sacred space, get started. You can make progress much faster than you think.

Come Home

My spirituality is not a fad or a phase. It means the world to me, and I build my life around the calm center of my being.

There are no shortcuts in the spiritual life. We waste a lot of time looking for quick fixes, for fast and easy ways to enlightenment. Progress begins when we make meditation and mindfulness a central aim of our lives and not just a fad or a novelty. We have to stop looking at the practice as a kind of sidecar to our real lives. We live only for this: to become more aware and awake. Everything else is a distraction from this central mission.

You may have dabbled in various different paths and philosophies in the past, but without putting your whole heart and life into them. All of that is in the past now. Let it go. In this place and time, strive to be only and completely in the moment. Surrender your willfulness, your ego, your thoughts and emotions. Lay everything aside and just be here in this space of refuge. Come home to yourself, come home to love, and come home to the teachings. Everything that you endured in the past has been leading up to this moment.

Life Preserver

When I feel overburdened in life, I go directly to my spiritual tradition, looking to the teachings to save me.

A drowning person might flail wildly, striking the lifeguard who is valiantly trying to bring the situation under control. A rope or a life preserver is a good tool for such a situation, because it prevents both the drowning person and the lifeguard from being drowned. The rope or the life preserver is the teaching that rescues us from our own panicked feelings. The lifeguard is the teacher or guru who can save us through detachment by having feet firmly planted. The one thing that the drowning person must do is calm down long enough to grab the rope. That one thing accomplished, the rest of life becomes possible.

When you are feeling stressed and worried, do you have the composure to be able to grab the rope of the teachings? Sit here in this place, and notice the frantic thoughts and the shallow breathing. Invoke the protection of the guru and the protection of your chosen divinity. Sit here in the stillness, and allow the turbulence to subside. Go deep within the inner space, and allow the world of the senses to recede. Wait here patiently for relief.

A Date with Destiny

I recognize that the feeling of guilt sometimes arises without any basis.
I refuse to be controlled by guilt, and I continue with my life's mission.

We often feel like our true selves don't get much of a chance to shine, because we expend so much energy just trying to pay the bills and keep things together. But we can allow ourselves a morning or an afternoon each week to realize our true goals. Maybe you dream of being a dancer, an artist, a writer, or a mathematician. You must steal time in order to make this happen, especially later in life, when so many responsibilities weigh so heavily. Don't ask permission; just sneak away to work on your projects.

You may find yourself feeling guilty when you work on projects related to your life's mission. Notice this guilt feeling and the thoughts that go along with it. Now analyze: does it really make sense to feel guilty about something that you truly believe is directly related to your purpose in life? When this feeling arises, inquire into its foundations. You will find it to be without support.

Older and Wiser

I ask for wisdom in all areas of my life.
I continue seeking wisdom as long as I live.

Whether we want to or not, we all get older. Hopefully we get wiser as well, but that part is not guaranteed. Plenty of full-grown adults act like spoiled children, always insisting on their own way. True wisdom doesn't arrive on a schedule, like a package ordered from Amazon. We have to set wisdom as a goal but never imagine that we have achieved it. We have to try not to get as ruffled by the inconveniences and setbacks of life, to learn how to thrive no matter what happens in the external conditions. We can't possess true wisdom; we can only keep seeking it.

After a few rounds of deep breathing, ask for true wisdom to come to you. Ask for wisdom in your relationships, in your working life, in your finances, in your use of resources, in your use of your body. See all of these areas of your life coming into harmony, no longer competing with one another. See all aims coalescing around the one goal of liberation from rebirth. See the one wisdom, present from before the world began, being made manifest in you. Become a jewel, reflecting the divine light.

Dial It Back

I need not perfectly control my own mind or perfectly control my external conditions. I simply make strategic adjustments here and there, subtly guiding my life toward Self-realization.

There is a lot of talk of mastery in the literature on spirituality and personal development. But this word, "mastery," sounds very intimidating and unattainable. Rather than seeking to master the mind or master our inner states, can we just influence them a little bit? So rather than trying to stop being angry, maybe we can just take the anger back a notch. Or instead of no longer craving X, maybe we can just work on reducing the craving at certain key junctures. If we think incrementally rather than in all-or-nothing terms, it becomes possible to find a way forward.

You may have been intimidated in your practice by thoughts of perfection. What does this vision of perfection look like for you? Can you imagine a less-than-perfect spiritual practice, one that takes into account your life the way that it is? One of the spiritual gifts (*siddhis*) is recognizing which practices will be most valuable in a given situation or in a given phase of life. What will be most effective, not in the abstract, but for you at this moment in your life?

The Illusion of Superiority

I do not use my position, my power, or my influence as leverage over others. I hold to my practices and beliefs, but I do not think that they make me better than any another person.

God doesn't judge things the way that human beings do. Class, status, ethnicity, religion, and all of the other markers of difference that matter from a human perspective do not matter from a divine point of view. Or, if you are allergic to theological language, think about whether these markers of privilege and difference are true from a scientific perspective. Scientifically, we are all distant relations, branches on the tree of life, all going back to the same trunk.

All of us have distinguishing features, but that does not mean that we have to view those distinguishing features as superior in some way. We must instead refuse to lord our unique characteristics over anyone, since every person has unique excellences. What attributes about yourself do you most value? What do you most want to project to the world? Without condemning yourself, can you imagine what it would be like to lose that most valued trait or characteristic? Can you imagine what it would be like to have a different set of values, to live in a different body?

Are You There?

I break out of the mental fog that prevents me from experiencing life directly. I catch myself drifting away, and I bring my attention back to the present moment.

We go through the motions of life but do not really attend to what we are doing. Mistakes are made, warning signs are missed. The little beauties and wonders go unnoticed as well. We let life pass by. We live as though in a fog, unaware of the world around us. This is what is called maya, or illusion—not only the feeling that we are separate from others but also the failure to connect with reality. Truly paying attention brings us to the unitive state in which we see ourselves as connected with everything in existence.

When does the mental fog descend on you most readily? When are you most distracted and out of touch? Today, try to do your practice during one of those most distracted times, say during the afternoon slump or the rush hour commute. Remember that mindfulness does not have to be anything more than deliberately paying attention to your surroundings with your whole self.

Heat and Resistance

I learn to generate the heat of austerity and guide it to the right places in my body and the right places in my life. I skillfully use this heat to cut the bonds that hold me to this life.

Suppose you bend a paper clip back and forth at the same point over and over again. Eventually, the weak point in the metal will get warm, and the clip will snap in two. It is the same way with all of our hang-ups and blockages: if we keep working them enough, they will give way and break. The bonds that hold us in place are temporal bonds and therefore subject to change. If we consistently apply pressure at strategic points, we can find release from all forms of limitation.

One of the Sanskrit terms for spiritual practice is *tapas*, which means asceticism or austerity. But it also means heat. Meditate now on the warmth of the body. As you breathe deeply, you will notice greater warmth coming into the body's core. You may even begin to sweat, especially when doing intense pranayama. See if you can guide and direct the body's heat, moving it up the spinal column and toward the crown of the head.

Get on the Train

I maintain awareness of my intended destination in life. I keep watch over my thoughts and feelings, my relationships and dealings, asking always whether I am moving in the right direction.

I learned everything I know about trains from New Jersey Transit. If you want to go to New Brunswick, make sure you are not on the Perth Amboy train. If you are going to Penn Station, it's okay to take the express, because it will stop there. During life we have to make sure that we are on the right train. We want to be on the "Peace Train" that Yusuf Islam (Cat Stevens) sang about, not the train to reckless despair. And we have to stay alert, so as not to miss the stop.

Do you know where your train is headed? This could be your train of thought, or your train car of friends and acquaintances. See your whole life as one whole undertaking. Do its overall tendencies lead in the direction where you want to go? What adjustments could you make so that your habits and relationships, your thoughts and emotions, align more closely with your intended destination?

Said and Done

I do everything that I can to ensure a good outcome for all of those affected by my decisions. But, at a certain point, I recognize that I must let go and let my actions speak for themselves.

There comes a time in any situation when we have said all that we know to say and have done all that we know to do. At that point we have to let go and trust that our efforts will be enough. We send our sayings and doings into the general flux of people and events. We wish our actions well and send them off into the world, in the same way that a mother bird must eventually watch her chicks leave the nest. We don't have the guarantee of success, but we do have a guarantee that our actions take on a life of their own. They become like independent agents as their effects unfurl.

Are you hanging on to a situation that has now passed out of your control? Name these places in your life where you have trouble relinquishing ownership. To help you let go, you might use a simple phrase like, "I have done enough." Practice releasing each place where you feel clingy and tense. See if you can put each thought to rest and dwell in this moment.

Beyond Belief

I have my cherished beliefs, but I recognize that no system of beliefs can take me all the way to the highest reality. I allow my beliefs to take me right up to the edge of the mystery, and then I stand in awe.

Whether you call God by the name of Hari, Hara, Jesus, or Allah, and whether you believe in science or theosophy or Buddhism or Judaism, you have a guiding framework of beliefs, a narrative used in order to make sense of the world. Human beings are creatures of ideas, and without these ideas we would be unable to take collective action, unable to construct an identity, unable to pursue meaningful work. As historical persons we must espouse some sort of belief system, but, at the same time, we have to look at these beliefs as provisional and not absolute. We use our beliefs to take us up to the edge of the unknown, and then we step into the mystery.

Take your contemplation out to the very edge of thoughts and words. Go to the place where there are no more descriptions, where there are no more labels. Look at the inner darkness: shades of red and black lit by lightning flashes. Gaze on the void. Do not attempt to tame it with definitions. Become another sort of creature, an ambiguous beast that no longer speaks in sentences. Leave behind all thoughts, even the most pious ones.

Cracker Jack Prizes

I practice skepticism toward promises of shiny objects at the end of a long struggle. I look to find my satisfaction in the present moment rather than at some unspecified time in the future.

Do you remember getting a box of Cracker Jacks as a kid, wanting so badly to get the toy surprise inside? The toy proved to be pretty disappointing in the end. Maybe it was a baseball card the size of a postage stamp or something equally as worthless. But it was a smart marketing gimmick: not only were you promised a little sugar buzz, but you were also given the suggestion that there would be a valuable reward for digging in. As we grow into adults, we still look for that prize at the bottom of the Cracker Jack box. We want another degree, a bigger house, or a beach body. It is as though we were still looking for that toy surprise. Only there is nothing there at the end of the striving or, at best, only a piece of paper.

What would you do if you reached your highest goal and found that it felt no different to have achieved it? Would you still go ahead with your plans, if you knew that you would feel exactly the same as before? If you cannot say that your pursuits are worthwhile even in the absence of a sense of having arrived, you may need to do some reevaluating. It is better to abandon the wrong plan halfway than to go through with something that you don't really want to do.

The A1 Slot

As a finite human being, I only have so much time. I will use my time to the best of my ability, to realize the best that I have in me.

In managing time, whatever goes in the A1 slot gets done, while everything else will be put on hold. Some of the lower priorities will get done sooner or later, and then an even lower tier of priorities will be put on hold until they die a natural death. That is why it is so important to be careful what we put in that A1 slot. Oftentimes, we unwittingly put web surfing and video games in the A1 slot, pushing everything else down the list by default. Nearly everyone gets distracted and goes off task: we just have to catch ourselves doing this and make sure that we put those things first that we really want to be first.

What activities most easily take you off task? Do you get distracted by checking email, eating snacks, or sending text messages? Or maybe you have more compulsive tics, like perpetual organizing or alphabetizing? See if you can set aside such behavior just for today while you work on your absolute highest priority in life.

At the Hour of Death

I look directly at my mortal condition, and I prioritize those things that I most want to do in life. I spend my days loving as much as possible, knowing that I may not pass this way again.

No one ever says on their deathbed, "I wish I had worked harder." Instead, people tend to think about their family and friends at the end of life. They tend to think about how they might have expressed themselves better or pursued some deferred dream. We might not be near death right now, but no one really knows when the time will come. It is probably impossible to be completely prepared, but we can start by making a choice to live fully at this moment, to stop deferring those things that we might have done.

When you die, what do you want people to say about you at your funeral? If you could make a list of adjectives that you would want people to use about you, what would they be? If someone were writing your eulogy, how would you want them to finish the sentence, "I remember that time when he/she . . ."? Without excessive striving, see if you can be a little more like that person you described.

Ancestors and Remembrance

I honor those who came before me, taking care to practice the lessons that they taught me. I open my heart in gratitude toward the past, which has made me what I am today.

My grandparents, who have all passed away now, were mostly mill workers, shopkeepers, and small-time farmers. They didn't live to see cell phones or the Internet, but I doubt their lives were at all lessened for lack of technological sophistication. I wonder what they would think of my work, which involves mostly doing things with words, since they mostly did things with their hands. I think they would be saddened by all of the political and economic divisions today, by the dividing of the world between blue collar and white collar, liberal and conservative.

Most non-Western traditions have some sort of veneration of ancestors. They do this to prevent spiritual pride and to acknowledge the continuing influence that the past has on us. Take a moment now to appreciate your ancestors. See them now, in your mind's eye, with both their good and bad features. Send love toward these people, whether or not you experienced them as warm or loving. Feel gratitude filling your mind and heart, and see the debt to the past being paid in full.

Understanding and Leadership

When conflict arises in my life, I take a step back to understand the situation. I place the burden on myself to understand the people in my life.

Life becomes easier when we meet people where they are rather than where we think they should be. When we try to understand the other person first, we can work with them much more productively. This is true no matter the nature of the relationship or where we fall in the power hierarchy. Teachers should try to understand their students, and students should try to understand their teachers. Supervisors should try to understand their employees, and vice versa. Genuine leadership comes from a place of mutual respect, not from a place of controlling and manipulating.

You may have one or more problem people in your life right now. Around these people, every conversation turns into an argument, and every little task becomes an occasion for grumbling. Ask yourself, "What am I failing to understand here?" Sit here in silent listening, genuinely searching for an answer. You may emerge from this experience with a slight shift in attitude or a small bit of insight that helps you to relate to this person better.

The Importance of Effort

I can have dramatic transformations in my life, but I have to be willing to give something in return. I set my will in motion, and my plans take shape.

In order to make it to a better place in life, we have to be willing to give something in return. We have to exert more effort, expand our networks, and pursue new ideas. The world can be an amazing place, but we have to do our part to make it happen, to make our own luck. It will do no good to complain about lack of opportunity, whether or not the complaint is justified. The universe simply favors action over inaction.

You may be thinking of places that feel stagnant in your own life right now. Perhaps a relationship with a spouse or significant other has gotten stale. Maybe you are having trouble attracting clients or customers. Maybe your home is looking a little more shabby than you want. When was the last time that you put serious effort into dealing with the stagnant problem in your life? Think of three things that you can do today to get that area of your life back on track, and take action right away.

The Divine Effulgence

I look for the faces of the divine in my own life.
I feel attracted to the divine names most suited to my situation in life.
I find the right keys to open the lock of my heart.

In the Hindu tradition, we have different deities associated with different divine qualities, Lord Hanuman for strength, Saraswati for wisdom, Lakshmi for wealth, and so forth. We go to the deities for help in our lives. People who come from monotheistic traditions may not have many deities, but they still have different aspects of God, like the ninety-nine names of Allah in Islam or the many different saints and the Trinity of Christian belief. These aspects of divinity help us to find the right form of intervention in our lives, like fitting the right key to a lock.

What images of the divine most speak to you today? What do you find to be inspiring and attractive? You may feel drawn to a particular saint or a few lines of poetry. Or maybe you take inspiration from something in nature, like a beloved forest or animal. Hold that image in your mind and sit in silent adoration. See if you can learn why you feel drawn to this particular source of inspiration, and find the lessons hidden there.

Every Day Is Day One

I abandon my concept of self and move into the flux of nature. I allow myself to become empty, so that I can merge with the forces of nature.

We can think of each day as a chance to start over. Whatever happened yesterday or last week, this day provides a new opportunity. You don't have to espouse the same beliefs that you did yesterday, eat the same foods that you did yesterday, or even be the same person that you were yesterday. This freedom from the past must be in place in order to make progress. You have to make a break with your habits and move in a new direction. When you are able to grant yourself this fresh start, you can reach new heights.

What you did, or failed to do, in the past does not matter now. In this space of calm abiding, release all thoughts of self. Let go of all feelings of personal identity, of likes and dislikes, of traits and personality. Let go of the need to prove yourself and the need to escape. Do not differentiate between yourself and this inner darkness. Become without qualities. Become nameless. Merge into your surroundings.

The Life of a Place

I live into the vibrant life of the places where I find myself.
I allow the rhythms of place to renew and refresh me.

Places have lives of their own: people coming and going, music flowing out of doorways, and street vendors, dog walkers, artists, punks, and freaks doing their thing in the park. Rural places have their rhythms as well: animals grazing, crops growing toward the harvest, and the cycles of work and rest. When we attune ourselves to places, we absorb their frequencies as they work their magic on us. The magic happens in the attunement, in being there. We come home to ourselves as we come home to place.

Try going out in the open somewhere today. It can be someplace bustling or someplace quiet. Feel the mood of that place, its rhythms and textures. Allow yourself to be absorbed into that place, to become a part of it. Feel yourself being taken away, taken into your surroundings. Become one with the scene, with the life unfolding around you.

Sprint versus Marathon

I look to the inner wellspring to find refreshment for my soul.
My heart leaps when I feel the divine being stir within me.

Sometimes life is a sprint, and sometimes it is a marathon. Sometimes we succeed by being fast and nimble, and sometimes we succeed by outlasting the competition. In the test of endurance, we have to look deep down inside ourselves to find the hidden reserves of energy. The human body, from the perspective of shakti yoga, is a conduit for energy, like a well that refills itself. Prana enters the body at the muladhara, or root chakra, and goes up the spinal column and through the crown of the head. So we can always look within in order to channel more energy, as we have an everlasting supply.

If you are feeling depleted today, do not worry. You have inside yourself the same energy that caused the big bang, the same force that propels rivers to the sea, and the same life that makes the flowers grow. Turn within, concentrate on the spinal column, and feel the energy currents moving up through the chakras. Picture this energy as all-sufficient, ready to heal your physical and emotional wounds, ready to give you inspiration and advice, ready to recharge your tired body and mind. Above all, trust very deeply in this primal energy, which is the source of all things.

Perseverance and Uniqueness

I see the divine in all things and all things in the divine.
I see the unique facets of my existence,
and I find in my own particularities an expression of the eternal.

Sometimes we all feel like we can't keep going, like the difficulties are just too much. And yet we survive. We face every single challenge bravely and keep going. Each person on the earth is a miracle in this way, in that we all keep going somehow. Admittedly some have it easier than others, and the world isn't fair in any normal sense of the word. But each life is a testament to the perseverance of our human nature, part of the drive of life toward greater fulfillment of itself. The uniqueness of each life makes each life valuable beyond measure.

You are the only person in the entire world with the past history and influences that you have. You are the only one with eyes of that exact luster, with a fingerprint with those exact whorls. You are a unique and indispensable manifestation of the divine nature, and, for that reason, you are holy. You deserve to be treasured, to be loved, to be fulfilled. Spend a few minutes treasuring your own unique nature, and marvel at the uniqueness of each and every thing in creation.

Love Unrestrained

I forsake altogether excuses and half measures. I leave behind me half-hearted devotion. I put my feet firmly on the path, and I will not grow weary.

We all have aspirations and goals, but are we willing to give them every last ounce of our effort? Are we willing to empty ourselves completely into the struggle? Are we willing to forsake all other goals and cling only to one cherished vision? If we don't reach the supreme goal, then it is because we only engage halfway. Or our efforts are so scattered and diluted that they can't come to fruition. So we have to be a little unreasonable, a little lavish in our pursuit of the beloved.

If your life has been littered with disappointments, do not fear. The way still lies open to you. At this point in your life, what could you see yourself doing without reservation, holding nothing back? Even now, as you sit here, put every ounce of attention into holding on to this present moment. Be completely awake and alert, letting nothing escape your notice. If you can be fully present to this moment, you can be fully present in any moment.

Clearing the Way

I inquire into myself for the reasons why I sabotage myself.
Understanding myself, I am able to make progress. I spring the traps that
I have set for myself, and I am able to continue along my way.

When we feel stuck in life, we usually say that we don't know the next step to take, that we have exhausted all of the options. Usually hidden in such a belief is an adversity toward taking some sort of risk that must be taken. We actually know what to do; it's just that we are unwilling to do it. We fear taking a big risk and falling flat on our faces. We fear looking like fools for going out on a limb with a crazy idea, which is much different than just not knowing what to do.

Why do you stop doing what you love? Answer this question, in detail, and you will see exactly how to improve your life. Only do not soliloquize: say it in one sentence or less. You will see the blockage in all clarity, which will also entail knowing how to remove the blockage. Don't overthink it: just see. You already know the way in your heart of hearts. Don't shrink back from it.

The News and the New

*I allow the news and the trends to blend into the background.
I take note of the developments in my own life and respond to
the leading edge of the present.*

The news isn't really new. There have always been crooked politicians, celebrity divorces, natural disasters, various human-caused tragedies. The human drama just keeps churning, over and over again, revolution followed by stagnation followed by decay, ad infinitum. It can be easy to get lost in the news, to feel insignificant or powerless in the face of the unceasing spectacle. There is nothing wrong with tuning out the news from time to time to focus on what is new with you.

You may feel humdrum today, as though everything in your life had remained exactly the same. But there are new developments in your life. Change is real, and it is all around you. See if you can notice something new right now, something in your life that wasn't there before, some change that came to you, intentionally or accidentally. Maybe it came as a result of your practice, or maybe you can't say why it came. The point is to notice, just to notice.

Beyond Stagnation

*I allow myself to move in new directions, regardless of success or failure.
I do not have to be the same person that I was years ago.*

When religions age, they become more rigid and dogmatic. Over time, these institutions forget the spontaneity and exuberance that led to their founding moments. The same thing happens to businesses, which gradually lose the entrepreneurial spirit and the drive to satisfy customers that characterized their early days. The same thing happens to each of us as we become victims of our success: we begin to stagnate and take things for granted.

Do you limit yourself to the self-concept that you had five or ten years ago? You may have changed as a person, but that doesn't necessarily mean that you are less effective or deficient somehow for having evolved. Practice looking at yourself the way that you are now, to include your embodiment, your habits, your thoughts, and your emotions. Accept yourself as you are now, and let go of expectations derived from the past.

Making the Most of the Time

Knowing my days to be limited, I spend the time living and loving.
I cherish my connections to all beings,
holding these loved ones in the space of compassion.

My dog Pearl, who is a black lab–Catahoula Cur mix, is now eleven years old. Her snout is turning white, and her eyesight is going. She has already had a cancerous tumor removed, and she prefers to spend her time outdoors, staring out at who-knows-what in the backyard. Aging and the passage of time becomes more apparent when we look at our companion animals. Doing so can serve as a reminder that our time, too, is passing, that we should use our days in the best ways that we can, by loving the people, animals, things, and activities in our lives.

These quiet moments are passing away, each one unique and unrepeatable. If you use a meditation timer, try to use each and every second to the fullest. With each passing moment, try to become more aware and awake. Let the daydreaming stop, and keep returning yourself to the present. Build the inner fervor for complete awakening.

The Full Stack

I regard all things in the universe as having their place.
I recognize the contribution of each member of the universal community.

Consider a stack of Jenga blocks. Each player pulls out one block as carefully as possible, trying not to wiggle the stack, until the unlucky moment when the whole thing comes crashing down. So it is with human societies and ecosystems. Each entity, living or nonliving, plays a part in keeping the whole thing standing. Remove one and the whole thing can come crashing down. So we have to be careful about making judgments of who or what is dispensable or important. We never know which entities are really bearing the weight.

Does your organization or your family have someone who is always the odd one out? Be on the lookout for the tendency to marginalize certain members of the groups to which you belong. Or are you relying too heavily on whoever is holding up the "stack"? Actively recognize the contributions of every member of your social circles. See the interconnections between every member of society and the connections between people and nature.

Alternate Futures

I craft the world of tomorrow with my actions today.
I build the world in which I want to live.

Regret is really an exercise in alternate possibilities: what would have happened if I had done X instead of Y? But it is really a futile exercise, because we have exactly the same present that we have. Instead, take that same what-if impulse and carry it over to the future: what will happen if I do X? This is still speculation, but it has the benefit of actually being possible, whereas regret is just completely beside the point.

You may be actively struggling with your possibilities for the future, or maybe things are pretty quiet right now in terms of your vocation and avocations. Hold open the space of reflection as you breathe deeply and expand the inner space. Ask for clarity about not only what to do as you move forward but also invite clarity as to how to go about your daily duties. Invite serenity into your life, and build yourself a foundation of peace in life.

Sharing the Light

I do not keep my insights to myself, but I strive to help others along the way wherever possible. I recognize that my fate is tied to the fate of every other being, and I view this entangled destiny as a great inspiration and strength.

We share the light of mindfulness when we smile instead of curse. We share the light of mindfulness when we assume some of the burdens borne by those around us. We share the light of meditation when we refuse to discriminate based on human categories of the understanding. We share the light of meditation when we practice constancy in our habits. We share the light of meditation when we rise above our limitations and cut through obstacles. We share the light of meditation when we hold our heads high, no matter how many difficulties we face.

Know that you have the light of consciousness within you today. Know that you have all of the intuition that you need today to live with fullness of purpose. Know that you have the joy and the peace that you need to overcome all negative states of mind. Know that you have the goodwill to make the lives of those around you brighter. Know that you have the tremendous power of self-transformation and world transformation. All of these things are with you now, and they will be with you throughout this day.

The Unseen Community

I belong to the unseen community of all beings. Each aspect of nature reverberates through me, and I belong to the mind of the universe.

We are not alone now, nor have we ever been alone. No matter how isolated we may feel at times, we still live in a shared reality that overlaps with those around us. We have commonalities with our fellow human beings, with nonhuman creatures, and even with ordinary matter. We are all a part of the undulating waves of change, the accretion and dissolution of things, the give-and-take of life and being. It follows that we were never born and can never die, as we belong to the fabric of the universe. Not even death can change this basic reality: we change states but never go away completely.

Dear one, you and I have no separation between us. This inner space is your temple and mine. The echoes of your thoughts echo through me, and I am your consciousness as well. We are all part of one body or one mind— call it by either name. Sorrow and joy are here: feel them. They are united in bliss, which is the union of all contrary forces.

The Nine Gates

I recognize my body as the vehicle that takes me through this life.
I recognize here subtle channels for prana, the divine essence
that takes me to the highest realization.

The body, in the Indian scriptures, is called the city of the nine gates. The gates are the openings in the body: the two ears, the two nostrils, the two eyes, the mouth, the anus, and the genitals. The body can be either a place of enslavement or a place of freedom, depending upon the attitude that we take toward it. As we learn the secrets of inner yoga, we view the body as a vehicle to higher states of awareness. We come to view the journey thus far merely as the preamble to a remarkable journey of self-exploration and inner awakening.

The teachings ever expand for those who are willing to ask. The infinite cannot be contained, so there is no limit to the process of awakening. What questions do you still have? What do you still want to know? Ask these questions now, and hold in your heart the firm intention of finding the answers. Resolve to continue growing until the city of the nine gates becomes a place of liberation.

Time in Motion

I purposely improve my relationship with time. I set aside procrastination and anxiety, and I treasure each hour as full of potential. I refuse to kill time, knowing that time holds the secret to my joy.

We measure time in conventional units of hours, minutes, and seconds, but time is still very mysterious to philosophers and physicists alike. We think of time like a material thing, like having a full tank of gas. We have plenty of time or not much time, we say. But time is more like a set of relationships than it is a material quantity. Time expands and contracts according to the priorities that we set for ourselves. We can have a good relationship with time, experiencing its passage as tranquil and beautiful, or we can have a bad relationship with time, in which we picture it like a malign force.

When you think of the passage of time, does it make you worried and anxious, or does it feel warm and inviting? Make peace with time by making peace with this moment and this day. What do you need to do today so that, when the day is done, you will be able to say that today was well spent? What do you need to do today to abide in peace? Go and do that.

Keep Exploring

I commit myself to unceasing exploration, both today and for the rest of my life. I will not rest content with what I have discovered so far, but will continue seeking, within and without, for as long as I live.

A year passes, a chapter ends, but the whole story has not yet ended as long as we are still alive. We cannot all be young in body, but we can be young in mind so long as we are willing to try new things, to go out and explore this beautiful world of ours. Just as the daffodils bloom each spring, our hearts bloom when we spring into motion. We can all do more and be more and engage more. This does not have to mean perfectionism or peak performance: we can just expand into new areas of life, new avenues of experience.

As you settle into your sacred space, imagine everything you know of the world to be a tiny speck in an ocean of milk (the Hindu creation myth). The ocean is churning to and fro, awesome in extent. You cling to the speck, because you know nothing else, but the ocean is vast and contains stores of both nectar and poison. Now imagine that a great tortoise or a great fish supports you, so that you can survey the ocean of milk. Imagine that the poison has been sapped from the milk, and that you can drink freely of nectar. You are seated firmly upon the cosmic ocean, which has been from the beginning of time. All that remains for you is infinite truth, infinite consciousness, and infinite bliss.

The End Is the Beginning

I yield to the passage of time, becoming more malleable with each passing year. I learn to work with time instead of against it, and, in this way, I prosper.

Time may be lived forward, but it holds recursive loops. You can learn from past mistakes and try to do better the next time around. You can approach the same situations with hope, a little wiser each time around. Each completion is a new beginning, a chance to start over with something new. There is a grace in starting over, in going around again. The wheel of the years, of the cycles and seasons, keeps turning, and we all turn with it.

Have you been working against time? Make peace with time today by making each moment, each hour, each day infinitely sacred and worthwhile. Strive to make every moment count, by being very efficient, yes, but also by packing creativity and love into each action. Leave the malaise of the past behind: depression and worry are done for you. Know that you have within you everything that you need to live a perfectly contented, blissful life.

Rituals for Strength

This present tension will pass. I work with renewed strength,
knowing that my illumination is near at hand.

It will do no good to be hopeless, to wallow in doubt in either the spiritual or material sphere. All of us must go on living, fulfilling our duties and purpose in life. It will be easier and more efficient to live with dynamism and strength than it will be to waver to and fro, in sadness and confusion. The more we exert ourselves, the quicker past karmas will be overcome, the closer the day of liberation. Even the most simple task, done with care and attention, is a ritual that shows your love and devotion.

This day, offer some flowers and fruit to your chosen divinity. The proper mantras are widely available online if you have never performed ritual worship. Allow your consciousness to become absorbed in the sacred words and gestures. Allow the presence of the divine to fill your home or office, and make your space into a temple.

For more information and further reading, see
http://anahatachakrasatsanga.org/bibliography/